The Stamp Art
and Postal History of

Michael Thompson &

Michael Hernandez de Luna

Cover credit: stamps, Michael Hernandez de Luna
Back cover: stamps, Michael Thompson

Frontispiece: Single stroke perforator, circa 1839

First American Edition
©2000 BAD PRESS BOOKS - CHICAGO

Edition of 5000

Creative Director: Michael Hernandez de Luna
Book Designer: Dorothy Mason
Copy Editors: Donna Jagela
            Micki LeSueur
            Paul Vriend
            David Bade

Library of Congress CIP data:

Thompson, Michael, 1951-
The Stamp Art and Postal History of Michael Thompson
and Michael Hernandez de Luna. 1st American ed.
Chicago : Badpress Books, 2000. 152 p. :chiefly col. ill.;
31 cm.
Includes introductory essays by the artists and others on
the history of mail art and stamp-making as art.
Includes bibliographical references.

ISBN 0967757215

1. Thompson, Michael, 1951 - 2. Hernandez de Luna,
Michael, 1957- 3. Mail art. 4. Postage stamps in art.
5. Postage stamps — Forgeries. 6. Mail fraud — Case studies.
I. Hernandez de Luna, Michael, 1957-

N6494.M35T456 2000

Printed in Korea

Contact information: B A D P R E S S B O O K S . C O M

CONTENTS

ACKNOWLEDGEMENTS

We would like to take this space to acknowledge and express our deep appreciation to the following individuals, who believed in us when we said we could publish this book, who patiently waited months to receive it, and whose generous financial support made the book possible.

Allan Pocius — Chicago
Ron & Maxine Linde — Arizona
JoJo DiCarlo — Chicago
Jane Kozuch & David Berten — Chicago
Chuck Thurow — Chicago
Dale Hillerman — Chicago
John & Adrienne Abrams — Connecticut
Candice B. Groot — Illinois
Nora Chiriboga — Chicago
Driek Zirinsky — Idaho
David & Terri Emory — Oregon
Andrew Bowdie — Oregon
Alexander Patterson — Oregon
Becky Keith — Chicago
Roy & Kathleen Reitz — Illinois
Jason Blake — Oregon
Jonathan D. Leitersdorf — New York
Mary K. & Thaddeus Staten-Long — Chicago
John Markin — Chicago
Carlos E. Pecciotto — Chicago
Dan & Mary Sutherland — Chicago
Umberto Ricco — Chicago
Tim Brown & Jill Ridell — Chicago
Lauren Moltz & John Clement — Chicago
Joseph & Anne Tabet — Illinois
Constance Hinkle — Chicago
Marla Mason — Chicago
Yves Klein Archives — France
Rotraut Moquay-Klein — Arizona
Daniel Moquay — Arizona
Robert Watts Archives — New York
Sara Seagull — New York
Larry Miller — New York
Richard Kateley — Chicago
Larry Yellen & Sue Fisher — Chicago
Aron Packer & Lisa Zschunke — Chicago
Clare Cavanaugh & Martin Murphy — Chicago
Mexican Fine Arts Center Museum — Chicago
Gretchen Rudy — Washington
Kevin Conway — Chicago
Nicholas & Dagmara Kokonas — Illinois
Morlen Sinoway & Susan Kavanaugh — Chicago
Robin Richman & Floyd Gompf — Chicago
Marilyn & Guy Revesz — Illinois
Suzanne Endsley — Chicago
Marcus Casa Madrid — Chicago
Norbert Zook — Chicago

A Stamp Collector's View

By Rob Haeseler, Sidney, Ohio

Word started to trickle in from Chicago during the winter of 1997-98 that two artists were getting in trouble with the postal authorities. Not since the 1970s when mail artists Anna Banana and Plastic Jack were married — by mail, of course — had there been a better story. I thought the readers of *Linn's Stamp News* would like to know what was happening. Here's the story I wrote for the issue of April 20, 1998. It was illustrated with several covers, the term which stamp collectors use for envelopes.

USPS sends ultimatum to Chicago artists: stop mailing fake stamps or be prosecuted. Postage stamps, it's often said, are miniature works of art. But are miniature works of art postage stamps? Two avant-garde artists in Chicago think they are, and that has landed them in hot water with the United States Postal Inspection Service. They have designed their own stamps, adding "USA" and "32," and have used them to mail envelopes, which they prize as works of conceptual modern art. Their realistic impressions pay tribute to everything that the Postal Service does not, including Congressman-turned-convict Dan Rostenkowski, whose stamp bears the legend "BUY, SELL, TRADE," and cigar-puffing mobster Al Capone (legend: "Big Al"). The more irreverent, blasphemous and bawdy the subject, the more likely they are to have produced an image of it and mailed it. Political boundaries mean nothing to them. They have created stamps for France, Germany, Italy, Mexico and Norway, and used them in those countries to send mail home. They are Michael Hernandez de Luna and Michael Thompson, graduates of the School of the Art Institute, Chicago. Covers which they've created now hang in art galleries around the country.

Linn's Stamp News Cover, April 20, 1998

How can these artists print their own stamps and use them on letters? Stamp collectors know that's against the law. Thompson and de Luna know it too. "We're pranksters, we're punks," says de Luna. For a long time they kept quiet about what they were doing. "We try to keep the Postal Service at arms' length," Thompson told an interviewer for *Metropolis* magazine. "I make a point of not knowing my mailman." But in 1995, the impulse to share something so unusual became overwhelming, and they had their first two-man show at the Oskar Friedl Gallery in Chicago. Titled "StampArt," it made page one of *The Chicago Tribune*. "Each of the 74 works on display . . . has fooled the U.S. Postal Service into canceling them as stamps, even though they depict subjects that have never been commemorated by the Postal Service, including Batman, Mao Tse-tung, the late Chicago Mayor Richard J. Daley or, in the more outrageous pieces, bare-chested women and condoms," the article reads. "It is that approval, at least as it passes in a blur through the maws of the cancellation and sorting machines, that Thompson and de Luna crave and what they say gives their work its value. Perhaps there is a bit of implicit critical respect on the part of postal officials. They say that although it is illegal, they do not intend to sweep in, raid the gallery and arrest the artists and imitators." That was in 1995; since then, their creations have been exhibited several times. And how is the art world reacting? "The response is phenomenal. People love the work," said Mija Riedel, one of the directors of a gallery in Mill Valley, California, a suburb of San Francisco.

Well, not everyone loves the work. Even though the Postal Service once tendered "a bit of implicit critical respect," it doesn't any more. Two Chicago Postal Inspectors with badges and guns paid Thompson a visit in February 1998. "This was no exercise in art appreciation," reported Chicago's *NewCity* weekly. "The Feds had arrived to deliver a message. Mail one of these again, they warned, and we'll prosecute you for felony mail fraud." A cease-and-desist order was also served on de Luna. Thompson recalled his encounter with the authorities: "They asked me if I'd ever copied one of their stamps. I said, 'Nah, you guys have your style and I have mine.' I'm done," he added. "The Feds can really mess up your life." De Luna told his attorney to deal with the matter. "They said we could make the fake stamps — that was no problem," he said. "I'm not a great talker, and I don't understand a lot about philately, you know," de Luna said. "Michael and me aren't the first to come along with a new idea. You've got millions of guys coming before us with their creation of arty stamps and illustrated covers. The difference is they used a regular postage stamp when they mailed them and we didn't."

Thompson and de Luna design their stamps using what de Luna calls "appropriated images" and what others might call piracy. It's not surprising that for every ten covers mailed, only two come back. Envelopes that were rejected by canceling machines were often handed over to supervisors who saw that they got to the Postal Inspectors. But in other instances, machine operators have canceled the rejected covers by hand and sent them on their way, silently endorsing anarchy. De Luna sees the canceling machines and their operators as the final step in printmaking. "They are included as a cohort in the art process," he says. Recently de Luna paid a visit to his local post office to buy some real stamps for invitations to an exhibit. A clerk showed him Alexander Calder commemoratives with their tiny images of free-form sculpture set against a stark white background. "I couldn't believe it," recalled de Luna. "I said, 'Hey, these really look like fake stamps.' They said, 'No, they're not. They're real ones.'"

As you read this book, notice the dates of the postmarks on the covers. Does it look like the creative impulse vanished with the warning from postal inspectors in February 1998? If anything, output has continued unabated, spurred on by demand from a growing audience of art collectors. Indeed, the latest miniature masterpieces of de Luna and Thompson bear the number "33" in recognition of the 33-cent first-class letter rate that went into effect January 10, 1999. Their art has always been faithful to the prevailing letter rate. Why hasn't the United States Postal Service made good its threat to give the artists a new home where they can apply their talents to making license plates? It could still happen, but it's probably not likely that they will be prosecuted. The attention paid to the two Michaels by the press has given them an aura of invincibility.

The Postal Service is concerned about what it calls revenue protection. In more serious cases involving the illegal reuse of stamps, it has acted quickly and decisively. During the 1960s and 1970s, for example, the Postal Service had trouble processing all its mail. Every day, high-speed canceling machines disgorged tens of thousands of envelopes without obliterating the stamps. Every night, businesses that processed credit card payments put their empty envelopes on the sidewalk to be picked up by trash haulers. But some unscrupulous scavengers gathered up the envelopes, soaked off the uncancelled stamps, dried them and resold them at a liberal discount. Most people don't know that a stamp which has carried a letter is considered to be used whether it has been canceled or not. The Postal Inspection Service uncovered several stamp-soaking schemes. In most cases, the perpetrators were fined or put on probation. It made good headlines.

But how would the public react to the news that two Chicago artists, whose work is being nationally exhibited, were hauled in for creating a few fake stamps lampooning the efforts of the Citizens' Stamp Advisory Committee? The Committee is composed of a dozen members drawn from the ranks of movie stars, prominent citizens and at least one stamp collector. Since the Cold War years of the Eisenhower Administration, the panel has been charged with deciding what subjects are fit to appear on the nation's postage stamps. The Postal Service's revenue protection argument really doesn't work with Thompson and de Luna. As long as they don't up the stakes too much, the government is probably going to leave them alone. However, any person, artist or not, who violates statutes regulating pornography in the mail might be hauled in on those charges, which have nothing to do with revenue protection. The longer the Postal Service puts off a final confrontation, the harder the job will be to justify the merits of suppression. The Postal Service has long been the butt of jokes, and this is but another joke, expressed with sophistication and greeted with appreciation by the viewers.

Although fake stamps have been around as long as real ones, there are different types of bogus issues. The more light-hearted are called cinderellas, or fantasy stamps, to distinguish them from postal counterfeits, which are created solely to defraud. The work of Thompson and de Luna is a blend of these: fantasy stamps to which denominations have been applied, suggesting legitimacy. You'd think an objective person could distinguish them from real stamps by their subject matter, especially when it's pretty outrageous. But this is not always possible because the Postal Service each year issues so many stamps, celebrating so many different subjects and causes, that postal workers cannot be expected to recognize them all. Nor are stamps visually inspected by letter sorters as they were in the days before mechanization. Today, many letter carriers do not even sort mail for their own routes, and so the faces of envelopes are often not seen until they arrive at their destinations. Only a stamp collector knows the amount of work involved in producing one of Thompson's or de Luna's covers. As much energy goes into assembling the component parts of each cover as is spent in producing the stamps that embellish them. De Luna and Thompson discovered that stamp shops and stamp shows are good sources for the materials used to create covers: old, unused envelopes with commercial corner cards, or return addresses, official government envelopes with the name of a federal agency, and airmail stickers, or etiquettes, as they are called by stamp collectors. Every stamp collector also knows that a good cover can be ruined by the Postal Service's high-speed canceling machines, which have a tendency to strip away parts of stamps as they cancel them. It's all part of the gamble — even mail is subject to the same grotesque destructive process. ∎

Rob Haeseler is a senior editor at *Linn's Stamp News*, the world's largest publication for stamp collectors, which is also on the Internet at www.linns.com

Artistamps and the Postal System
A Background to the Postal Activities of
Michael Thompson and Michael Hernandez de Luna

By James Warren Felter, Vancouver, Canada

An artist has always been involved in the production of postage stamps; after all, someone has to create the image, select the colors and design the stamp. The problem for the artist is that when working for the postal system he is constrained by subject matter, selection committees, politics, etc. The artist's solution to these difficulties is to issue his own stamps. These have come to be known as "artistamps," a term coined by the late Canadian artistamp activist Thomas Michael Bidner (1944-1989). Many postage stamps are considered miniature "works of art" and actually introduce millions of young collectors to major works of art from museums around the globe. Artistamps are works of art. They are made by artists to express their creativity, to decorate their mail and to exchange with other artists. They are not designed or meant to be sold as prepayment for mail delivery. Like any work of art, they carry a message — one the artist has chosen to communicate. "The stamp is a symbol which takes possession of the imaginary," writes French art critic Pierre Restany in his essay *"The Artist's Stamp."* He goes on to explain that the artist who decides to utilize the postage stamp format creates an imaginary territory in which he can, with the greatest freedom, express his artistic vision of the way things are. The universally recognized format of the postage stamp gives the artist's vision a sense of authority and authenticity that has been sanctioned by some "higher" authority.

The first postage stamp (known as the Penny Black) debuted in Great Britain in May of 1840. Twenty years later in Canada, Postmaster General Charles Connell of Woodstock, New Brunswick, replaced Queen Victoria's likeness on a brown 5¢ postage stamp with a picture of himself which he believed "would please the people." Such pseudo postage stamps can resemble "real" stamps, and often cause confusion.

In 1898 the European powers stepped into the civil war raging on the Mediterranean island of Crete. The island was declared an autonomous republic. During the year of occupation, the British, French, Italian, and Russian forces on the island issued their own postage stamps. Soon forgeries began to appear. Francois Fournier of Geneva, Switzerland had manufactured some of the British occupation issues. Fournier is well-known for printing copies of famous stamps. He often advertised these copies in leading newspapers and considered himself a benefactor to the average collector who could not afford the genuine article. From comparisons of the perforation of the authentic British stamp with the forgery, it is clear Fournier had manufactured both.

Sometimes recycling discarded postal material may be the only way to continue making art. The German artist Karl Schwesig (1898-1955) was working, it is believed, for the armed Communist French Resistance Movement when he was captured in 1940. He was placed in one of the largest internment camps of World War II, Camp Gurs, which was located in the foothills of the Pyrenees close to the Spanish border near Pau in unoccupied Vichy, France. Schwesig had been listed as one of the degenerate artists who were blacklisted for their style, subject matter or political activity

Courtesy of the Artist and the FIVE/CINQ Archives

by the authorities of Nazi-occupied France. His citizenship had been revoked and his property confiscated by the Nazis in 1937. In Gurs, Schwesig found himself without sufficient art supplies. International relief agencies such as the YMCA donated some musical instruments and art supplies to the inmates, but there was not enough to go around. Schwesig found the selvage (margin) of a stamp sheet. On this perforated bit of paper he drew a series of mock postage stamps in colored ink. 21 of his "GURS" stamps depict men, women and children surviving the conditions of the camp: mud, lice, black marketeering, poor clothing, lack of food, epidemics and inevitably, death. Three large stamps commemorate the "Liberty, Equality and Fraternity" of the camp while a fourth air mail stamp depicts Uncle Sam as an eagle flying into the camp carrying a relief basket. Two exhibitions were presented at Gurs during 1941. Schwesig managed to escape in 1943.

A few artistamps were created after those of Camp Gurs, but it wasn't until Yves Klein, the French New Realist painter, performance artist, and conceptualist, created the "Blue Klein" in 1957, that the art form was brought to the attention of the media. Klein had discovered a unique color and named it "International Klein Blue." He painted over regular postage stamps with his new color and affixed them on 3,500 postcard invitations to his exhibition "La vide" (The void). The French postal system canceled the stamps and delivered the invitations, which caused a scandal. It was later learned that Klein had previously reached an understanding with the French postal authorities. He had paid for the postage necessary to mail his invitations and tipped a postal clerk to cancel his Klein Blue stamp on the invitations.

In the U.S., Robert M. Watts (1923-1988), one of the original members of Fluxus, produced SAFE POST, K.U.K. FELD POST and JOCK POST stamps in 1961. These were included in a postage stamp dispensing machine mounted to the wall in Watts' exhibition "Constructions, Objects, Events and Games" at Grand Central Modern Gallery in New York City during the same year. Watts' most famous and most widely reproduced artistamps were the YAMFLUG 5 POST and the FLUXPOST 17-17 sheets of 1963 and 1964. He issued these editions in sheets of 100 stamps on gummed and perforated paper, with a serial number in the bottom corner. Watts' technique was collage with unexpected, sometimes surreal or erotic, images printed using the photo-offset lithograph process. Producing his stamps in this manner allowed Watts a far wider distribution than stamps of earlier stamp artists, and he integrated his stamps as completely as possible into traditional usage. As early as 1962, they were successfully substituted for U.S. postage stamps on envelopes delivered by postal carriers. "Flux Post Kit 7," one of the Flux Boxes designed by another Fluxus artist, George Maciunas, contained artistamp sheets by various artists including Watts and Maciunas, Fluxpost rubber-stamp cancellation mark and Fluxus postcards. Many of these were distributed internationally through the Fluxus network of correspondents and artists. Watts' Fluxpost stamps were also made available to the public at the Pace Gallery in New York City in February of 1964.

In 1968, New Zealand artist and printer Bruce Grenville and a group of fellow anarchists set themselves the task of creating an extraordinarily convincing illusion of the existence of the "Sultanate of Occussi-Ambeno." Occussi-Ambeno is the name of an area on the northwest coast of the island of Timor. It disappeared from the map after Indonesia invaded East Timor in 1975. Grenville and his co-conspirators created a history dating back to 1848 and established diplomatic relations with such states as Monaco and Liechtenstein. Occussi-Ambeno began to issue its own postage stamps. Convinced of the existence of the Sultanate, a European consortium headquartered in Spain contracted with the Sultan, Michael Ismail the First, and with Occussi-Ambeno's relevant postal authorities to supply the Sultanate's postage stamps. Considerable amounts of money changed hands and soon large, colorful Occussi-Ambeno stamps appeared in stamp markets around the world. Eventually the consortium realized the true nature of Occussi-Ambeno and canceled the contract. But Grenville continued to create Occussi-Ambeno stamps,

r,
enue,
B.C.,
3

Courtesy of the Artist and the FIVE/CINQ Archives

using his own designs and commissioning designs from other artists. His issues expanded to include the States of "Sedang," "Fantippo," "The Sultanate of Upper Yafa" and "The People's Democratic Republic of Kemp Land." Grenville's stamps continue to cause confusion. The *Evening Standard* of Palmerston North, New Zealand, reported in a front page article on October 1st, 1999 that "Police are investigating what appear to be fraudulent stamps released to celebrate the Palmpex stamp exhibition running in Palmerston North this weekend." The stamp pictured in the article is an Occussi-Ambeno 90-cent commemorative.

In 1970, American artist William Farley made an enlarged photocopy of one of the first U.S. postage stamps. It was a 10-cent issue depicting the face of George Washington, the "Father of His Country." Farley, upset with the political situation in the U.S., replaced the head of Washington with his own, ponytail and all. Instead of his face, Farley showed the back of his head, symbolically indicating that the "Father of His Country" has turned his back on his children. One of the gummed, perforated, 2.5 x 3cm. black on white offset stamps was used to mail a letter to Farley's mother in Phoenix, Arizona. It was delivered by two FBI agents and the ensuing investigation led to Farley. Accompanied by his lawyer and a tape recorder, Farley met with FBI agents and after some discussion, Farley was asked to turn over all remaining copies of his stamp to the FBI. Farley complied.

Further north, Vincent Trasov, one of Canada's pioneers in mail art, was sympathetic to the Fluxus artists in New York and Europe and in 1972 he created a prepaid 8-cent "Canada Post Card" at the Coach House Press in Toronto. The card and the stamp image replicate the official prepaid 3-cent Canadian post card of the early '30s, except that the 3 on the King George VI stamp image has been subtly changed to an 8. Some of the post cards were overprinted with "FIRST DAY OF ISSUE" while others had the overprint "FAKE COLLAGE by Ray Johnson." Approximately 100 of the post cards were mailed to artists involved in the emerging "mail art network" in April, 1972. All were canceled by the Toronto Post Office.

The death of Andy Warhol led to another important event in the history of artistamps and the postal system. Upon hearing of the American Pop-artist's untimely passing, Parisian artist Michel Hosszú created a limited edition of 2,500 stamps, 25 sheets, each different. The sheets were printed in the Warhol mode, using silk-screen with a six-color scheme. The image Hosszú placed on the stamps is a miniature recreation of a 1967 Warhol self-portrait. The text below the image reads simply: "Self-portrait, 1967, ANDY WARHOL, 1930-1987." The stamps were produced without denomination or country to permit them to be posted

anywhere in the world. After perforating the edition, Hosszú tore up 9 sheets and affixed one stamp to each of 900 envelopes. These were then mailed without any actual postage stamps from 30 countries around the world. The stamps are a homage to Warhol, and the process of posting them to friends, art dealers, collectors, curators and museums was Hosszú's worldwide performance piece, dedicated to making Warhol more well-known internationally. While posting letters without sufficient, or any, postage being paid might be considered illegal, postal services from Tahiti to Kuwait honored the stamps.

In 1994, Canada Post issued an unusual sheet of postage stamps: the 43-cent stamp has a white circle in the centre. The full mint sheet provided gummed disks of the same size as the blank circle, with various designs and text for different occasions such as birthdays, or weddings. One could stick any of the printed circles over the blank white circle and post them. Hearing of this led the master stamp artist known as Dogfish to act quickly in producing a commemorative stamp in celebration of his 43rd birthday. In his capacity as Post Master General of Tui-Tui, an independent "5th State" surrounded by the city of Seattle, Dogfish drove from Seattle to Vancouver, Canada to purchase 500 copies of the Canadian stamp. He then used a letter press to print his own Tui-Tui designs onto the blank circle. Three hundred were used on First Day cover envelopes and posted from Canada. As far as can be determined they were delivered without incident. This is the only known artistamp which is also legally valid for postage.

The relationship between artistamps and the postal system, despite some welcome exceptions, continues to be a bit uneasy. Creators of artistamps have always used their stamps to decorate their mail and this has caused few problems with postal authorities. Recently in Canada, Anna Banana, a leading light in artistamp production, was told by two postal clerks in two different post offices that she could not affix her artistamps to the upper right hand corner, where the postage stamp is supposed to be placed. Anna and other artists have been putting their stamps in the upper right corner of their packages and letters for years and then affixing the correct postage next to them. This causes the franking machines to cancel both the artistamp and the real stamp. A postal clerk objected to Anna's envelopes because, he said, "some people are mailing things with such 'stickers' and not paying postage." Anna explained she intended to purchase and use the correct postage as well, and that she had been mailing her letters this way for a long time. Another clerk remarked that he was "surprised someone hasn't reported you for it."

Within the last decade of the twentieth century, philatelic museums in Europe and the Americas have begun to acknowledge and collect artistamps. In 1993, The Musée de la Post in Paris presented a major exhibition of artistamps, curated by French stamp-maker Jean-Nöel Laszlo X. The following year in Bern, Switzerland the PTT-Museum (now the Museum of Communication) presented another exhibit organized by Swiss artistamp makers H.R. Fricker, Günther Ruch and Manfred Vanci Stímemann. These museums now

Courtesy of the Artist and the FIVE/CINQ Archives

have permanent collections of mail art and artistamps. Since then, the Canadian Postal Museum within the Museum of Civilization in Ottawa has joined in collecting artistamps, and exhibits selected ones on their Internet web site. In July of 1998 the Museo de Filatelia de Oaxaca, Mexico, opened its doors. Six months later, an exhibition and three-day conference entitled "Mail Art towards the New Millennium" was organized. The positive reaction to this event has led the museum to develop a permanent place in its collections and activities program for artistamps and other mail art ephemera. ■

Contemporary North American artist Jas W. Felter created the first exhibit to examine the phenomena now known as artistamps in 1974. He is also the creator and director of the Jas Cyberspace Museum (www.faximum.com/jas), which contains a large International artistamp Gallery. Jas lives and maintains his studio in West Vancouver, British Columbia.

Pushing the Envelope: Mail Art and the Michaels
By Simon Anderson, Chicago, Illinois

Some of the best art I have experienced has arrived through my letter box, and some of the worst. I've had poems, pictures, periodicals, pornography, profundity, platitudes and pap. Correspondence art covers a spectrum of quality and style, created by a range of people with manifold intentions, and very often for no reason at all. A relatively recent addition to the panoply of artistic media, Mail Art is a term for the surprisingly wide variety of objects, ideas and activities, connected by their use — or misuse — of the international postal service.

Michael Hernandez de Luna and Michael Thompson address many of the concerns associated with correspondence art. Apart from the obvious postal connection, the project-based structure of their collaboration combines the humorous, political overtones, the illicit and impish tenor of their pranks and their deceptively casual aesthetic to provide an ideal opportunity to reflect on the salient points and signal developments of correspondence art.

Mail art has a complicated and as-yet-unfolding history, still to be written, despite praiseworthy attempts. Current orthodoxy holds that the activity became popular through the 1960s; although Bern Porter — fertile and long-lived progenitor of the medium — staked his claim to history when he declared that he began to make art as communication on Tuesday, November the 11th, 1914, and the game of when-who-sent-what-to-whom-and-why could set the limits to pre-date the Penny Black. Communication systems are supposed to explain indented and whittled bones dating back to the Paleolithic era, and any comprehensive history of a correspondence aesthetic would have to additionally account for a wide array of art-at-a-distance, from the Kula Ring of Melanesia by way of Richard Fairbanks' Boston tavern to www.ekac.org. There have been scores of global surveys exhibited and collected; volumes of magazines have been privately published and distributed; large archives exist in major museums, and made-for-mail art works, such as Elinor Antin's "picaresque photo-novel" *100 Boots* frequently featured in the catalogue of several international art dealers. Both Thompson and Hernandez de Luna present a sophisticated twist on this variegated history, combining the random markers of official passage with a deliberate manipulation of the aesthetic involved; their small-scale prints, connected to the much denser history of printmaking, dovetail at various points — including teamwork, political humor and tricksterism — with the fragmentary origins of art-through-the-mail, as this brief survey hopes to indicate.

Historians of the medium such as Mike Crane argue that the historical impetus for mail art was essentially threefold, coming from Fluxus, Ray Johnson, and Nouveau Realisme. A more encompassing proposition would be that individuals as geographically, temporally and temperamentally different as Marcel Duchamp, Yoshio Nakajima and Mr. Peanut (alias Vincent Trasov, one of the Canadians attached to Image Bank, who dressed as the character from Planter's Peanuts and ran for Mayor of Vancouver on an aestheticist platform in 1974) among a legion of others — have used the mail to realize the pleasure of fruitful camaraderie and the value of a network, as well as the thrill of subversion. It is, however, only since access to rapid and cheap international postal systems — air mail began in 1918, and the first semi-automatic, multi-position letter sorting machine, known as the Transorma, was introduced into the American Post Office in 1957 — combined with the advent of equally affordable, simple and speedy reprographic media that such actions, ideas and collaborations have been published and disseminated widely enough for the "attitude" that constitutes mail to become visible.[1]

The combination of favorable conditions in technology, social development and aesthetic freedom which gave rise to mail art coincided happily with the career and reputation of Ray Johnson, who first achieved prominence in the no-man's-land between Neo-Dada and American Pop Art. He had a legendary status as prankster up until his suicide in

1995. His reputation as a prime shaper of mail art tradition was foretold by a review in the first-ever issue of New York's *Village Voice*, of his 1955 exhibition at Orientalia Bookstore, which mentioned his prodigious mailing list. His immortality was later ensured by the publication in 1965 of *The Paper Snake*, a careful rearrangement of Dick Higgins' collection of mail art from Johnson, which also announced the public fact of the New York Correspondence School of Art (NYCS) — a chimeric edifice whose cod-corporate identity was hugely influential on subsequent generations.

The Paper Snake revealed aesthetic possibilities within the limits of postal regulations; Johnson, by virtue of delicate little contraptions to set off the reflexes of newly acquired tastes was able to play the mail "like a harp" and make a lively, funny, and beautiful tune.

On April 5th, 1973, Johnson informed the "Deaths" section of the *New York Times* that the NYCS had died, in a letter ostensibly signed "Buddha University," heir apparent. Despite this, the NYCS lived on in Johnson's growing mythology, having a clear influence on such collaborative projects as mail art proselytizer and Fluxus genius Ken Friedman's "Sock of the Month Club," and a more than nominal effect on the New York Corre Sponge Dance School of Vancouver — a concept by the tremendously influential collective Image Bank; or the *NYCS Weekly Breeder*, one of many efforts by Bill Gaglione and Tim Mancusi in the early 1970s.

Since the end of World War II, European collaborations had existed almost entirely as postal communities, such as the French College du Pataphysique [founded in 1948] which was a virtual school, replete with a baroque bureaucracy of satraps and superintendents. Ersatz corporations, surreal organizations, and officious-sounding organizations have continued to abound since the late 1950s, covering the gamut from Ace Space to "zaj" — a Spanish group which found a different way to exploit the means of the delivery system to their particular ends, by organizing a postal concert in the winter of 1965. Such coalitions as these constitute a correspondence art heritage which must include the variety of communities-at-a-distance founded by Asger Jorn, and the more formal association of Nouveau Realisme, of which several artists, such as Daniel Spoerri, made great use of rubber-stamps. The most cohesive — if not coherent — of these groups, and the most central to any history of mail art is Fluxus, the international coterie of experimenters, poets, musicians, players, artists, happeners and clowns who were named in 1962.

Because Fluxus was internationally dispersed from its beginning in the late 1950s and early 1960s, it was inevitable that the mail art played a large part in its development. It existed as a mutable anthology of mail art, made visible through editions which tend to be small, light, and even designed for posting. Mail-order was intended to boost sales, and was the only method of selling the material in periods when there was no retail outlet. In a pattern which was to become a norm, many Fluxus artists met for the first time via the post office.

Robert Watts first became known to Fluxus' coordinator George Maciunas through the mail, sending him post cards with inlaid explosive devices ("Hospital Events," 1963) when Maciunas lay in a Wiesbaden, Germany sick room. Watts, a very prolific artist, had already initiated a number of events through the post, including some with George Brecht on the occasion of their two-year-long Yam Festival. The two artists collaborated on many actions, projects and events, many of which relied on the mail for success. Making energetic use of the aesthetic properties of the post, whether exploiting the subtle shades of manilla or effectively and excessively rubber-stamping text and image, the pair also mailed a surprising and varied collection of everyday household, office and hardware items, as part of a "Delivery Event." This early network occasionally involved an unknown or random audience who could receive an equally serendipitous object through the post, by simply sending one of several quoted sums of money, determined by chance, naturally.

Watts, who had a lifelong interest in philately, and made provocative use of his stamp collection in his work, also gave a lasting contribution to mail art by virtue of his creation of unofficial — fake, that is — postage stamps, mass-produced in sheets which often shared

SAFEPOST / W.C. Fields, *Robert Watts*[2]

a theme — although the imagery ran the gamut of popular culture. Like both Thompson and Hernandez de Luna, Watts was blessed with a wry and clever sense of humor, and again as our two contemporaries, he repeatedly and deliberately targeted politics, power, sex and popular culture in numerous collections such as Safepost, Jockpost, Yam Flug, and Fluxpost. He made his multiples available through the Fluxus mail-order warehouse, as well as via vending machine, appropriating a commercial stamp dispenser to sell the miniature offsets, one or two at a time, for a few cents. Also like the two Michaels, Watts illegally substituted his own stamps for those of the U.S. Postal Service, and subsequently framed those envelopes which successfully sneaked through the system.

Later, with Ben Vautier and Ken Friedman, Watts developed a Maciunas-design "Flux-Post-Kit" complete with rubber-stamps, Fluxpost stamps and post cards. The kit embodies many aspects of the confluence between Fluxus and mail art, including The Postman's Choice. A simple post card, identical on both sides, no image, just two spaces for stamp and address; the only message being "The Postman's Choice" repeated on both sides in English and French. Having addressed, affixed stamps and posted the card, its destination — its very fate — is entirely in the hands of the sorter or postman. This mixture of chance and anonymous whim is exactly the reliance shared by Hernandez de Luna and Thompson; dependent on the people in the system, the human face of the "Big Monster" of the international postal system.

Alongside Watts, Fluxus gathered a constellation of deities into the mail art pantheon; Ben Vautier produced a large number of postal works, including a correspondence festival, of "non-art, anti-art/truth-art, how to change art and mankind" (1965). He also mailed out a sporadic newsletter and disseminated other hilarious and pointed concepts from Nice, France; even attempting to direct-at-a-distance the multiples which Maciunas published in New York.

There were many Asian connections to Fluxus — again, associations assisted by mail — including Takako Saito, who conceptualized many delicate pieces for Maciunas, among them a proposal for post cards to be included in Fluxpack 3. Fellow Japanese artist Mieko (Chieko) Shiomi instigated several mail-driven "Spatial Poems," published by Maciunas. These world-wide correspondence projects took several forms, although the process followed a recognizable structure. The participants were, apart from her many international pen-friends, all those on the Fluxus mailng list, and their reports were published as diaries, maps and books. Spatial Poem #1 consisted of a world map made of cork, with pinned flags to document those places which her correspondents reported placing "the word or words" which she asked them to write and deposit. Spatial Poem #2 was a second map, this time simply documenting the compass direction which her large cast of correspondents were facing at a particular time and place, and Spatial Poem #3 took the form of a calendar, noting the actions of an overlapping and intercontinental collection of artists at certain times of the day on certain days. Other versions included rolls of microfilm. In all there were over ten Spatial Poems, four of which were published by Fluxus. As a method of working — initiating a project which was dispersed via air mail, returned through the same system, then gathered, collocated and published, with results being once again entered into the postal network for distribution — individuals collectivized by Fluxus made use of the mails as a medium, or, as some artists claim, as a support, for their ideas.

Many mail artists believe themselves to be part of an "eternal network," a term which owes its use primarily to yet another Fluxus associate, Robert Filliou. A one-time economist who dropped out to invent and develop new concepts in art and poetry, Filliou — again in collaboration with Fluxus maestro George Brecht — coined the phrase "eternal network" to describe the widest field of mail art activity. In 1965, he moved to Villefranche-sur-Mer with Brecht, where they opened their shop La Cedille qui Sourit, the first of a number of "Centres of Permanent Creation" founded by Filliou. La Cedille existed to invent "everything that has or has not been invented" and under these auspices they produced an enormous variety of concept artworks, including a number of "suspense poems," which arrived by post in installments. As seen in their subsequent book *La Cedille Qui Sourit,* they also conceived and took part in numerous telegram and letter games throughout their stay. When financial exigencies brought about the dissolution of the partnership, consolation came from their shared concept:

> There is always someone asleep and someone awake,
>
> someone dreaming asleep, someone dreaming awake,
>
> someone eating, someone hungry,
>
> someone fighting, someone loving,
>
> someone making money, someone broke,
>
> someone traveling, someone staying put,
>
> someone helping, someone hindering,
>
> someone enjoying, someone suffering,
>
> someone indifferent,
>
> someone starting, someone stopping,
>
> only the network is eternal — the network is everlasting.

Filliou revived the term, as part of other collaborations during the 1970s, with several teams of Canadian artists: General Idea; Image Bank and W.O.R.K.S., each which added decisively to the concept, until the "eternal network" has become a widely-accepted moniker for some kinds of correspondence art.

Every Fluxus artist took part in some mail art exercise, but not every mail artist was or has been a Fluxus artist: the field is a good deal wider than any single or simple influence, and mail art contains other heritages, other networks, other aesthetics. On the East Coast of the United States, postal activity was given a different definition by the subversive and poetic activities of Wallace Berman.

Contemporaneous with Johnson and Fluxus, though scarcely touched by them, Berman was a Los Angeles pool-hall hustler whose sexy and surreal drawings of vanguard jazz musicians ended up as album covers. Although he matured into an almost uncategorizable artist who wielded a wide influence, and a gentle family man who produced thoughtful and beautiful objects, he mellowed but never really grew out of the vital themes of his early years: dope, women and cool. In an act of equivalence worthy of Filliou, Berman — a collagist, early photocopy artist and home publisher — declared that "Art is Love is God." In 1957, he was arrested and fined $1000 for obscenity after including a semi-abstract drawing by the beat poet Cameron in his first — and only real — exhibition, held at the Ferus Gallery. After this bruising brush with the law, he moved to San Francisco and spent several years in self-imposed exile, widening his circle of correspondence to include Jess (collage artist), Dennis Hopper, and David Meltzer, among others, and establishing himself as one of the most important visual poets of the West Coast scene. Clearly connected to West Coast beat culture — itself a shifting and well-travelled network — his made-for-the-mail art periodical *Semina* nevertheless made bold, lyrical and gorgeous statements which demonstrate the gestural and aesthetic possibilities of the mail, despite its regulated system. Every issue — maybe every copy — was different, and depended on the postal services for completion as well as distribution: *Semina 9*, the final issue, consisted of a small, illustrated envelope, the cover and the mailer being the same, carrying a single-page poem by Michael McClure.

Berman's seemingly casual design style was deceptive; after accepting and acknowledging material limits defined by resources (found paper, "beat" type) he labored over each decision of precise placement before committing works to the random attentions of the postal system. Not only do Thompson and Hernandez de Luna share with Berman this rich, dense, and carefully careless aesthetic, but they also rely on our familiarity with, and fascination for, the marks of the mail process. Furthermore, our almost unconscious tendency to read the collage of rubber prints, enigmatic codes and official or unofficial stamps as a journey, as a visually expressive testament to survival of a passage through enemy territory, is common to all three. Although it would be hard to categorize Berman as a prankster, both he and his work represent a subtle and subversive element, an underground connected by attitude, and directly or indirectly, through the mail.

Yves Klein, best known signatory of the Nouveau Realists, and most famous perhaps for his identical blue monochrome paintings, also moved art toward pranks and projects with concepts such as the "Zone of Immaterial

Pictorial Sensitivity"; an invisible and experiential art work which simply left evidence: a receipt. To purchase a Zone which varied in size and cost, one needed to offer a given weight of fine gold, half of which was to be thrown in the sea in exchange for which one was given a signed receipt detailing the deal, half of which was burned. Klein additionally furthered the cause of mail art proper by posting invitations to his most notorious introduction of the Zone with a hand-made stamp of International Klein Blue, passing as an official affiche. These illicit aspects continue as important strands in the thread of correspondence art, whether in the outrageous nature of the project, as characterized by Pauline Smith's "Adolf Hitler Fan Club" or Bum Bank's pioneering homoerotic anthologies, or in the parody of exchanging artworks for postage.

Pranks, impious japes and heretical projects as art have been around since Alfred Jarry and have accompanied the mail since the earliest days of organized delivery. Because the best pranks "evoke a liberation of expression...and challenge the authority of appearances." Since Picabia's copy of Duchamp's altered da Vinci's Mona Lisa, they have cropped up repeatedly on the dark side of the artistic avant-garde, from Jorgen Nash through Joey Skaggs to Stewart Home. At one end of the tradition lie Hernandez de Luna and Thompson's cleverly presented envelopes, representing a scandalous transport from Japan with stamps honoring deadly cult Aum Shinrikyo, or the slyly obscene commemorative to the Marquis de Sade, invoking a steamy passage from Paris to Michigan. In a slightly different vein, Genesis P-Orridge — whose notorious pranks include an allegedly fictional insertion into a published index of contemporary artists — was put to trial and fined for mailing obscenities in a case whose vigorous defense, aided by testimonials from a roster of artworld notables, is detailed in the publication G.P.O. vs G.P-O (General Post Office vs Genesis P-Orridge). Between these there is a wide territory: from Bruce Connor mailing greetings to fellow Bruce Connors of America on his birthday, to Don Celender's published responses generated by his conceptual propositions. Celender described wildly offbeat but vaguely plausible schemes to international corporations and institutions, asking for support or sponsorship: replies varied from incomprehendingly polite to patronizingly amused. These examples reveal another element common to mail projects: serendipity.

Although it is not at all supposed to be a matter of luck that mail arrives, no system is perfect: the first level of chance lies there. Next, addressees may or may not be receptive and, of course, people move. Above that, mail artists often deliberately play with fortune: a decorative envelope is at the whim of many men and machines, and even when the stamps are official and sufficient, many obscure regulations apply. Furthermore, some pranksters choose to operate at a high level of chance, either challenging official sanction or developing methods to build randomness into the work. Robin Klassnik instigated works by "losing" thousands of envelopes in the streets of London, each asking the finder to return them enclosing a specific kind of item; e.g., yellow and plastic. All those returned were combined into a sculpture, entirely composed by the fortuitous choice of unknown contributors. In the rather more serious situation of the oppressive Czech regime, Milan Knizak mailed Fluxus-like performance instructions to strangers whose names were taken randomly from telephone books. Testing different laws on a different continent, using a similar method, Sam's Cafe — a trio of artists who offered an MA in Rubber Stamp Art — were arrested but finally acquitted in 1971 after mailing out bills for $76.40 to 20,000 San Franciscans.

This apparent delight in the game links numbers of otherwise disparate types, as does the inevitable target of many postal pranks: the Post Office. One artist who theorized this guerrilla activity and participated in it at a memorable level was Ulises Carrion, a Mexican who lived and worked in Amsterdam, although his influence spread as far as the postal system. In 1977, Carrion, who was by then also a well-known proselytizer, collector and maker of artists' books, founded The Erratic Art Mail International System (E.A.M.I.S.), one of the above-mentioned innumerable artist-organizations which bloomed throughout the decade. E.A.M.I.S., an informal structure of non-postal delivery methods, was one of Carrion's weapons against oppression; against the "Big Monster."

Mail art knocks at the door of the castle where the Big Monster lives. Every invitation we receive to participate in a mail art project is part of the guerrilla war against the Big Monster. Every mail art piece is a weapon thrown against the Monster who is the owner of the castle, who separates us one from the others, all of us. The Big Monster can take

multiple forms and might be rattled in manifold ways. From the profound yet understated ambitions of veteran and eternal networker Bern Porter of Maine:

"Say multiple things in variation leaving the core a bang
Jar, upset and kick the teeth of the mail art people who touch it
Calm the nerves of the final beholder"

to the tragi-comically cosmic assault on eternally monstrous mortality waged by Italian G. A. Cavellini, who saturated the address lists of the world with auto-hagiographic stickers, stamps, posters and catalogues printed by the thousands and all distributed by mail. In some places the enemy was truly Big and Monstrous. In Czechoslovakia, Knizak, now a famous veteran from the cultural front of the Cold War, was the focus of a mail art sponsored, world-wide appeal for mercy after his arrest and sentencing on charges of obscenity, accusations which were naked disguises for his real crime of political difference. In Brazil, Paulo Bruscky and Daniel Santiago's *Segundo Exposicao International de Arte Correo* was censored and prohibited by the police, who held the organizers prisoner for three days — despite the official support later given to Arte Postal only five years later in the 1981 Bienal de Sao Paolo. In Uruguay, the disappearance of mail artists Clemente Padin and Jorge Caraballo became the focus of Geoffrey Cook's postal work "The Padin/Caraballo Project," and in Poland, the

Monster's castle was buried so deep in an ideological forest as to drive prolific mail publisher and activist Pawel Petasz to finally abandon his metiers, xerography and rubber-stamp art, in favor of ball-point pen and regulation-size paper, because "printing is the field of state's enemies activity, if not the official and legal press."

Elsewhere, the Monster, not quite so Big, was merely the machine politics of the provincial gallery world, whose castle was likely to house a museum. For many mail artists of the 1970s and early 80s, there was a much debated opposition to the conventions of the art establishment, which gathered adherents under the simple banner; "No jury/no fee/no returns." This slogan, appended to countless invitations to participate in exhibition, publication or project, meant that any contribution would be accepted without censorship or favor, free and unrestricted, conditional only that all work could be kept by the organizer/gallery and thereafter regarded as his/her property. When this rule was occasionally flouted, an international outcry reverberated through the network, and the exhibition might be boycotted. "Mail art projects fit gallery scenes but usually strain them enough to permanently change their shape" wrote David Zack, later active around the 1990 art strike — another complex correspondence jape. Curators and publishers became staging-posts for temporary shows which moved on after exhibition. Mammoth address lists, begun by enterprising groups such as Image Bank or General Idea, and by prolific individuals like Ken Friedman or Klaus Groh, took the place of catalogues, and were amended and passed on freely. Mail art periodicals appeared which served as mobile cradles for new projects.

Rather than regarding the mail as an artificial vehicle for completed projects, these phenomenas tended to promote their incorporation of the postal service into a way of working. They range from serial publications such as *8 x 10 Art Magazine*, published by Ely Raman, who relied on invited contributors to provide 200 or so copies of a page, which he collated and distributed by mail, to Aart van Barneveld's publishing house, "Stempelplaats" which among a variety of projects issued its own stamp-oriented periodical *Rubber*. Each edition, each act, operated as a chunk of information posted onto the network, visual, conceptual, and detail-rich. There is no typical issue of *Rubber*, but many contained close to 100 addresses, including links to *Commonpress*, begun in 1977 by Pawel Petasz. *Commonpress* was a thematic, serial publication whose executors changed with each issue. "The editor selects the theme, size, deadline and reproduction process for the issue utilizing his/her abilities in a personal and unique way." It consisted entirely of participant-contributions and appeared in a surprising variety of physical forms with a large array of themes and acted as some kind of prototype of virtual publication in its shifting of content, audience, and concept, plus both centre and parameters. This essay can represent only a fraction of the torrent of periodicals and projects spawned throughout the next decades, and for every magazine there was seemingly an exhibition, for each project an anthology, and more calls for images, ideas or stamps-as-art.

The story of stamps-as-art has blossomed and diversified in parallel to that of correspondence art in general. It includes the American E. F. Higgins III, whose "Doo-Da" stamps are transferred from transparencies of his paintings to color xeroxs on gummed paper, and who in 1977 organized the First New York Stamp Invite, a collection of 24 stamps designed by as many artists; it includes Ian Hamilton-Finlay, who created his own commemorative issues — celebrating then-unrealized Scottish independence — in his own unique style; it includes H.R.Fricker, a Swiss artist whose 1989 catalogue from Kunstverein St. Gallen is profusely illustrated by color reproductions of the envelopes, stamps, and rubber-stamp impressions which form the visual aspect of his work. His stance might easily be determined from the title of his 1987 publication *Mail Art is not Fine Art: It's the Artist Who is Fine*. Fricker was, however, one of the organizers of the "Decentralized Worldwide Mail Art Congress" which began in 1986, and he reveals his connections to mail art history by his correspondents and commentators, who include Monty Cantsin, Pawel Petasz and Vittore Baroni, among others, returning us to the eternal network.

Ray Johnson issue by E. F. Higgins III from a portrait Higg did of Ray in 1997. (8.5" x 11," 30 stamps) ©2000

With links and connections between individuals, coalitions, institutions and ideas multiplying exponentially, it becomes necessary to imagine recombinant histories and flexible permutations of style — perhaps prefiguring Internet attitudes. Correspondence art is still too fresh to be clear, still barely open to traditional historical analysis; it remains sufficient only to include rather than exclude. Theories of communication merely skim across the surface of this densely woven phenomenon; the light of history penetrates only so far. As one anonymous stamp declared, "The medium is the misunderstanding: the misunderstanding is the message." What is visible enough to connect these heterogeneous groups and individuals is an attitude. An attitude rather than an aesthetic; the presence of wit instead of a particular style of humor; political tendencies as opposed to ideological positions.

Thompson and Hernandez de Luna certainly have the attitude, and mail art's fragmentary story is discernable in their work. They combine the wicked stamp, the tasty sheet, the oblique story of the passage written across the envelope. Wolves in the attire of officialdom wielding the language of art: the picture, the post office, and the prank, the tongue that licks the stamp stays stuck out too long before retrenching firmly into a wide-grinning cheek. ∎

Simon Anderson is an Associate Professor of Art History, Theory and Criticism at The School of the Art Institute, Chicago. He is an artist and a cultural historian who has written about Fluxism, Situationism and Artist's books.

1   "Correspondence art is not a movement, not an -ism… " Mike Crane "A Very Brief History and Definition of mail art" Artists Books and Bookworths ex. cat. Experimental Art Foundation Adelaide, 1978. p.3

2   ROBERT WATTS: SAFEPOST / W.C. FIELDS / Published by the artist in 1961.

3   ROBERT WATTS: FLUXPOST 17 / Published by the artist in 1964.

4   ROBERT WATTS: JOCKPOST / Published by the artist in 1961.

5   ROBERT WATTS: YAMFLUG 5 / Published by the artist in 1963.

The Stamp Art
and Postal History of

Michael Thompson

The Stamp Project and its Consequences

By Michael Thompson, Chicago, Illinois

The idea of making stamps was the result of a missed opportunity. I read an article concerning the publication of the Doonesbury comic strip in the form of four postage stamps, complete with perforations, denominations, and "USA" printed on each panel. Readers, it turns out, had carefully cut out the panels, perforations and all, pasted them on envelopes, dropped them into a mail box, and they were delivered with cancellations. It seemed a brilliant joke, a subversion of the system of taxation, with someone else's representation. It was a wonderfully inappropriate act but one that I missed and promptly forgot. Weeks later I was leafing through a popular weekly news magazine and came upon another example of a faux stamp. This one represented Bugs Bunny, again complete with cartoon perforations, the 25¢ denomination, the "USA," and the ears extending beyond the perforations. Perfect...fate was giving me an opportunity to participate in this wonderful gag. I carefully cut around the perforations and the ears, affixed the "stamp" to an envelope, addressed it to myself and dropped it into a mail box. Two days later it was delivered, complete with a cancellation. I was hooked. What else could be used as postage, I wondered?

DOONESBURY © G. B. Trudeau. Reprinted with permission of
UNIVERSAL PRESS SYNDICATE. All rights reserved.

Courtesy of the Artist

I began appropriating small, stamp-sized images, sometimes placing the picture on top of another stamp to give the impression of perforations. I would use Christmas seals, adding the denomination and "USA" with press-type letters. A miniature deck of nudie playing cards provided a salacious tint to the fun. Matchbook covers proved to be the right size so I began collecting old interesting matchboxes, soaking off the labels, gluing them to envelopes, applying the Letraset letters right onto the image and dropping it into the mail. The first few years of the project were confined to these one-of-a-kind stamps, the images determined as much by their size as by any other factor. Michael Hernandez de Luna joined the undertaking in 1994 and suggested creating sheets of stamps using a color copier, a development that added a new conceptual boost to the scheme. Multiples increased the chances of success and provided that wonderful matrix of Pop Art, the grid and repetition.

The post office processes millions of pieces of mail daily. Their size and automation have been an important factor in the success of our project. Still, the rate of our success amazes me. We offer these stamps for consideration, into the jaws of this sophisticated corporation which tags their stamps with fluorescent inks specifically to identify fraudelent stamps. They have in place procedures for detecting bogus stamps, reused stamps or insufficient postage; these are stamped return to sender for additional postage. I can count on one hand the number of envelopes that have been returned for insufficient postage or charged postage due at the other end. It is certainly possible and probable that given the lengths to which we go to obviate the nature of our stamps that there is occasionally a collaborative aspect to the project. When an envelope arrives festooned with cancellations, commemorating, for instance, large mammary glands, does that argue a willing participation? It certainly gets one wondering. Though there have been exceptions to that rule. I once made a Norwegian stamp using a reproduction of a painting by Gustave Courbet called The Origin of the World. It was painted in 1866 and offering a rather frank view of a woman's genitalia. When the letter to which it was attached was posted in Oslo, the Postal Authorities discovered it, took offense and contacted Postal Authorities in Washington, who in turn contacted the Chicago Field Office, who contacted me. They knocked on my door one day. I was expecting Chicago Building Inspectors that day to do an annual inspection of my studio and when I opened the door one of the two rather officious individuals asked if I was expecting them. Thinking that they were the city inspectors I answered that, yes, I'd been expecting them. They informed me that they were U.S. Postal Inspectors and were interested in discussing my stamps; could they come in? Disregarding the advice repeatedly tendered by my attorney, my overriding curiosity prevailed and I opened the door. The visit lasted over an hour.

Courtesy of the Artist

They were young, a man and a woman, armed but disarmingly casual, possessing a generous sense of humor and an extensive knowledge of the stamp project. They asked to see the work. As they looked through the books I keep the stamps in, they mentioned how they had versions of this or that stamp, chuckled at another and tossed a question at me concerning my friend and fellow traveller Michael Hernandez de Luna. The atmosphere ebbed between their seemingly weary chagrin to ominous threat, alternating from conviviality to consternation. They referred to their attendance at all our previous shows, to their burgeoning collection of our work, and finally to the consequences of continuing to produce the work, which included possible violations of the following federal laws, as defined by the United States Code: 18 USC 501 (counterfeiting), 18 USC 502 (postage and revenue stamps of foreign governments), 18 USC 1463 (mailing indecent matter on wrappers or envelopes), and 18 USC 1725 (postage unpaid on deposited mail matter). Additionally, I was informed that I was in possible violation of Illinois state law, 720 ILCS 5/16-3 (theft of labor or services or use of property). The meeting ended with the delivery of a Statement of Voluntary Discontinuance to be signed, notarized and returned via the enclosed stamped and addressed envelope. Needless to say, I now refer all official communications to my attorney.

This was a project that employed all the tools of tradecraft; couriers, cut-outs, drops, aliases, spurious documents, disguise, safehouses...and we too were hiding in plain sight, our stamps rarely subtle, often oversized, begging discovery. We flaunt our excesses.

When I stumbled upon the notion of making stamps, I had no idea what would become of these perforated bits of paper or the thorny issues that would arise from this mere parlor game. I would discover a landscape replete with federal and state statutes, Postal Inspectors posing as patrons at art openings and electronic sensors designed to ferret out fraudulent intent. The idea which began as a lark became a campaign. My appreciation of the ramifications of this hobby and the realization that, as official documents, stamps provided an opportunity to propagandize, co-opt the "line," insert my own message and have it canceled, and delivered, grew proportionally with the success of the work.

The final irony about this project is the fact that both Hernandez and I have been awarded Artists Fellowships by the Illinois Arts Council in recognition of our outstanding work and commitment within the arts, and we were granted those awards on the basis of this project. The cynic in me allows that the state is just giving us the rope to hang ourselves, that while one agency within the state is enabling the project, another is preparing to prosecute us. It's the classic good cop, bad cop scenario and, as with most continuing stories, you'll have to tune in to see how this one ends. The following pages portray an elaborate subterfuge of global proportions. ■

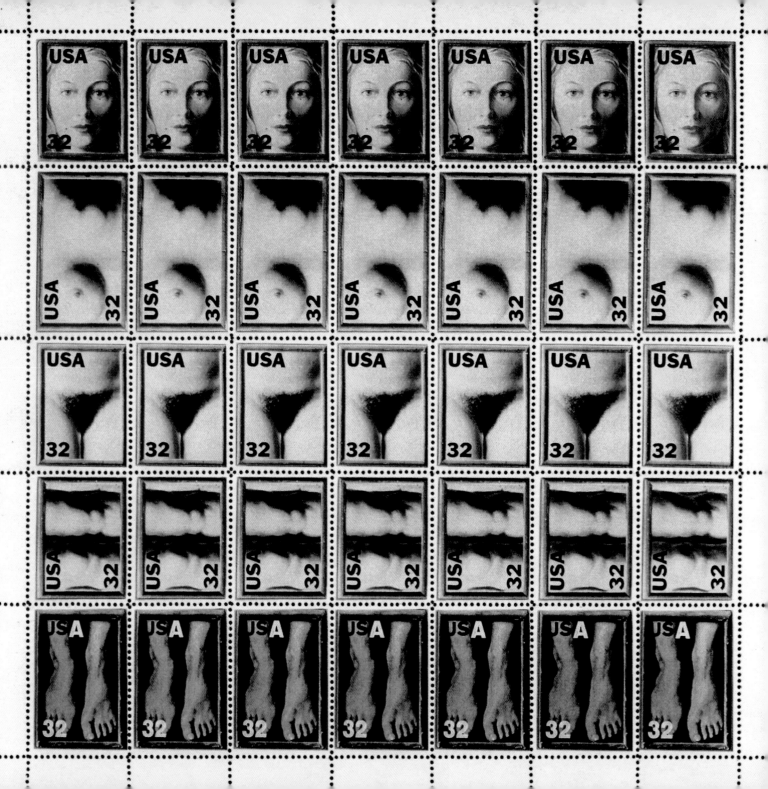

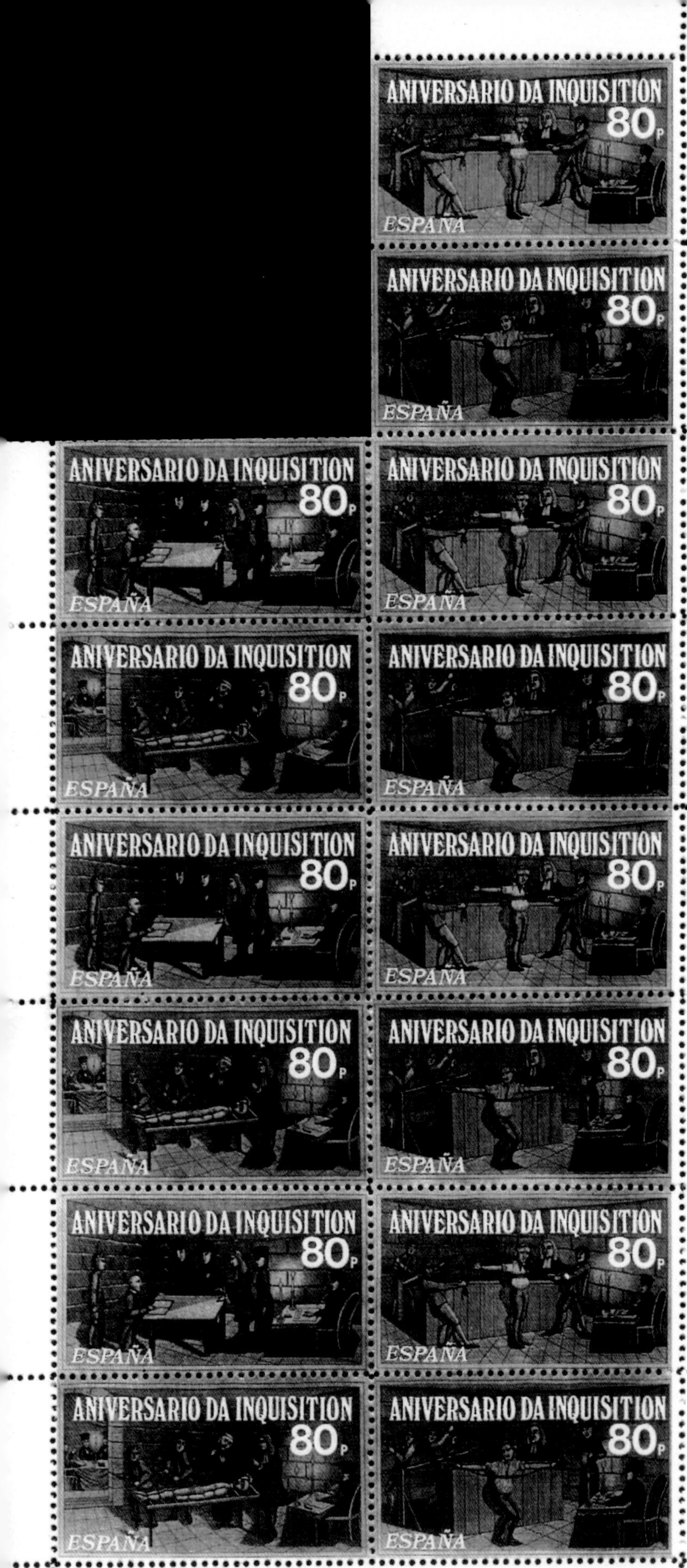
ANIVERSARIO DA INQUISITION
80 P
ESPAÑA

Aniversario da Inquisition — 1998 — Spanish cancellation

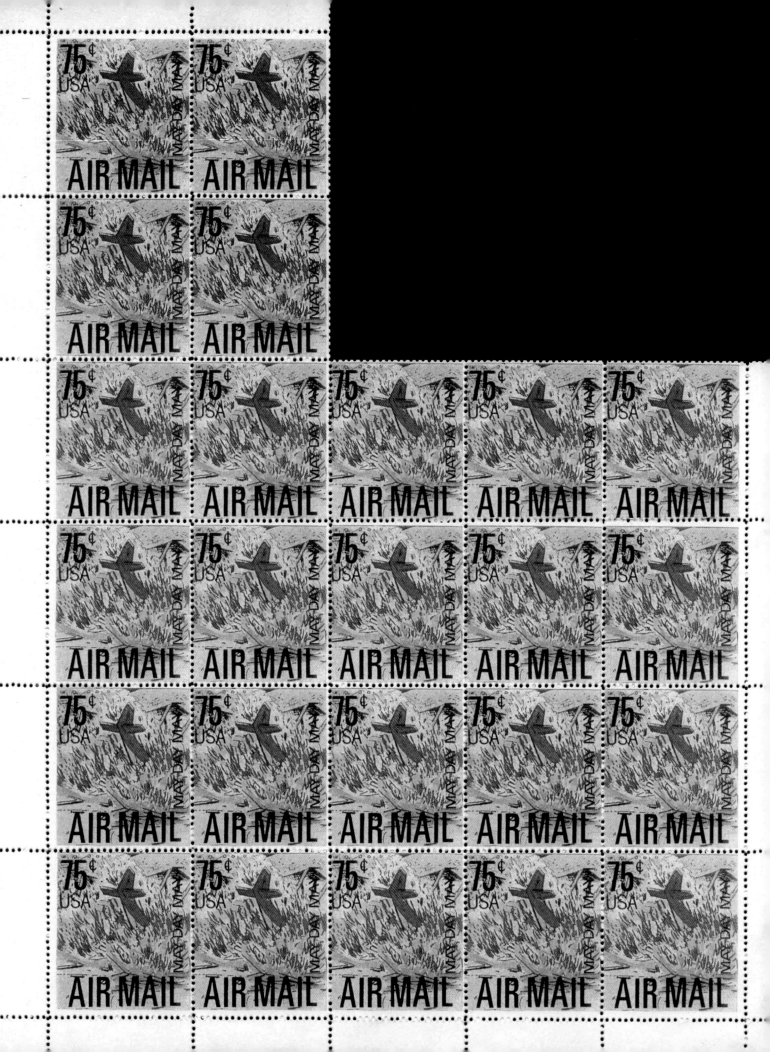

Received in damaged condition

75¢ USA AIR MAIL — MAY DAY MAY

75¢ USA AIR MAIL — MAY DAY MAY

75¢ USA AIR MAIL — MAY DAY MAY

ПО ВЪЗДУХА
PAR AVION

ПО В?
PAR

or Current Occupant
1259 W. Fry

USA 32¢
HUNT DEER

12132
Chicago, Illinois
60612

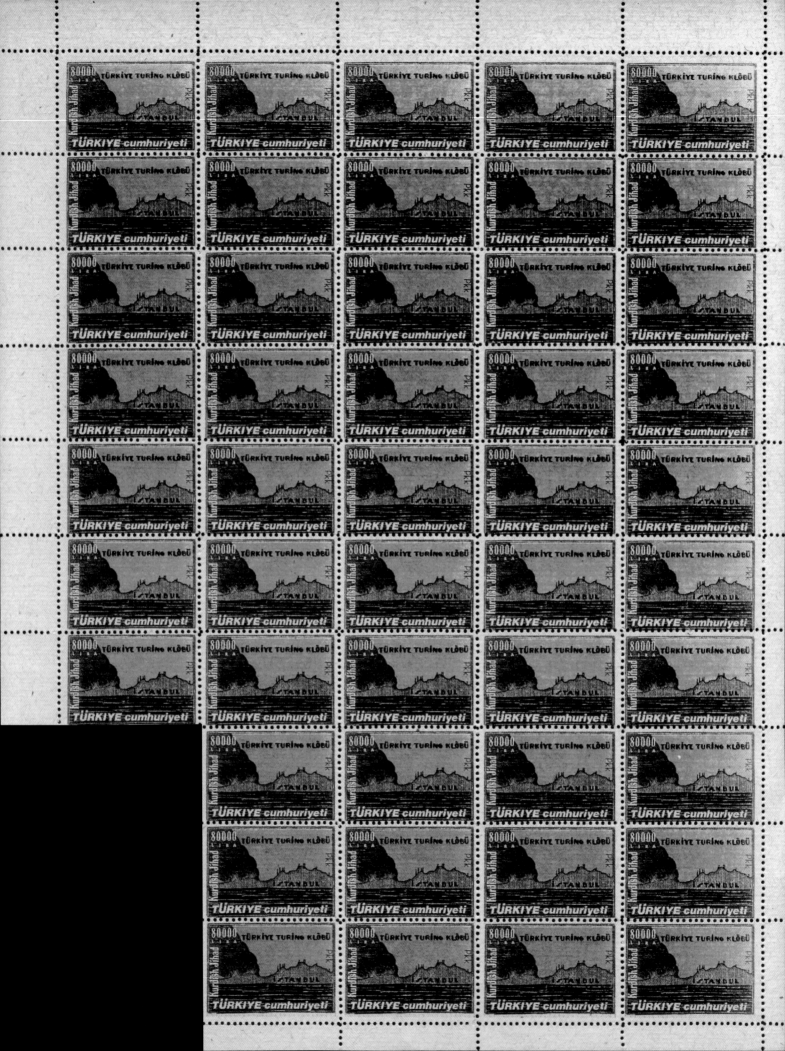

34

TÜRKIYE cumhuriyeti
Pkk
İSTANBUL
80000
TÜRKİYE TURİNE KLÜBÜ
Kurdish jihad

28.8.99
DALYAN

MR. MORLEN SINOWAY ATELIER

2035 WEST WABANSIA AVENUE

CHICAGO, ILLINOIS 60647

UNITED STATES OF AMERICA

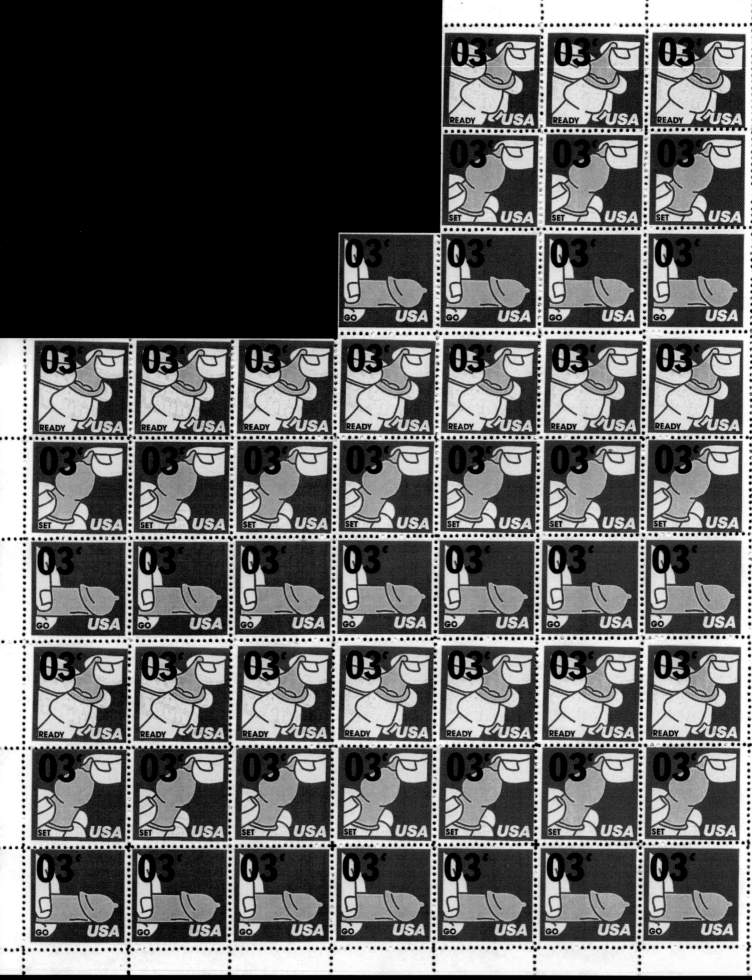

36

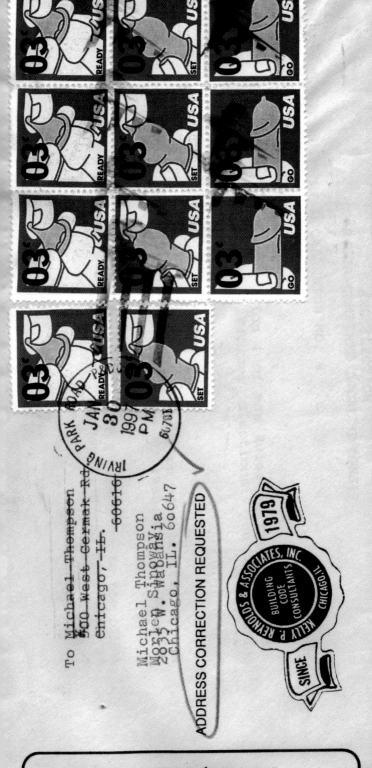

To Michael Thompson
500 West Germak Rd
Chicago IL 60616

Michael Thompson
2835 W. Harlem Singapuria
Chicago, IL 60647

ADDRESS CORRECTION REQUESTED

IRVING PARK JAN 30 1997 PM 60701

KELLY P. REYNOLDS & ASSOCIATES, INC.
1979
BUILDING CODE CONSULTANTS
CHICAGO, IL
SINCE

CODES & STANDARDS®
833 WEST CHICAGO AVENUE   #200
CHICAGO, IL 60622-5406

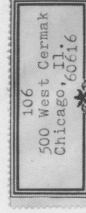

32 CENTS

U S A

fords theater

IRVING PARK RD P&DC IL 606 · PM 03 APR 1996

106
500 West Cermak
Chicago, Il.
60616

Written from
DINKLER-TUTWILER HOTEL
BIRMINGHAM 3, ALABAMA

Return in 5 days to

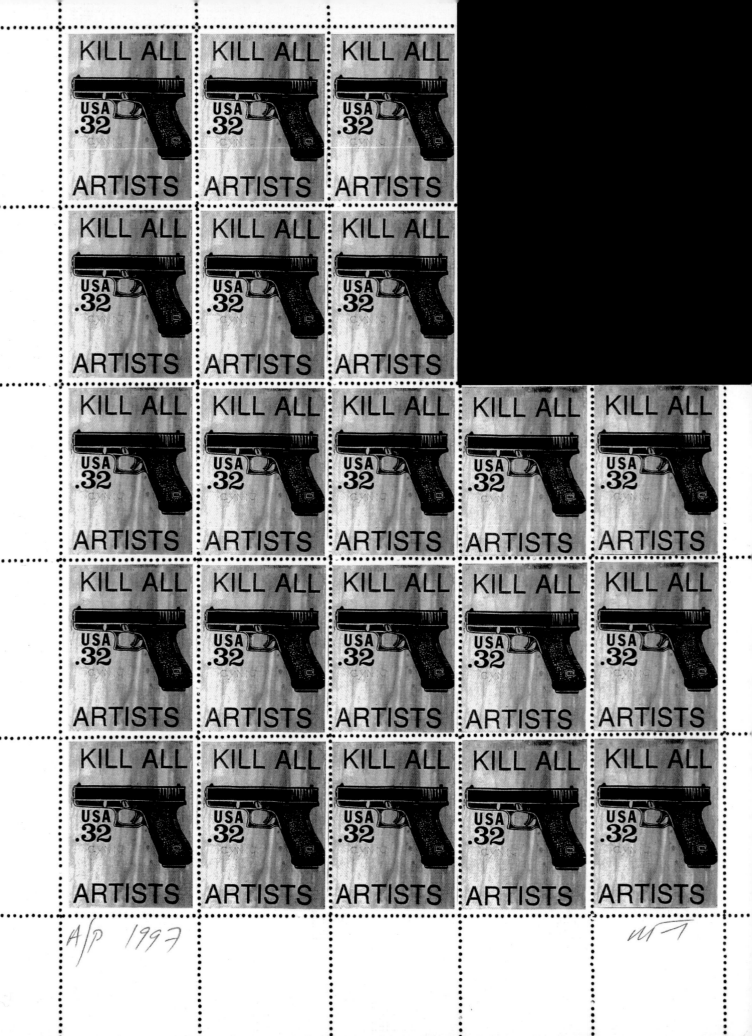

A/P 1997

46

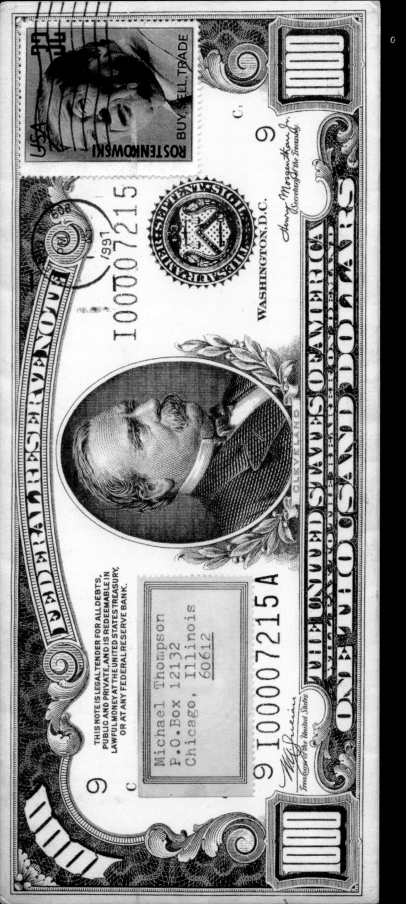

...owski (Buy, Sell, Trade) — 1997

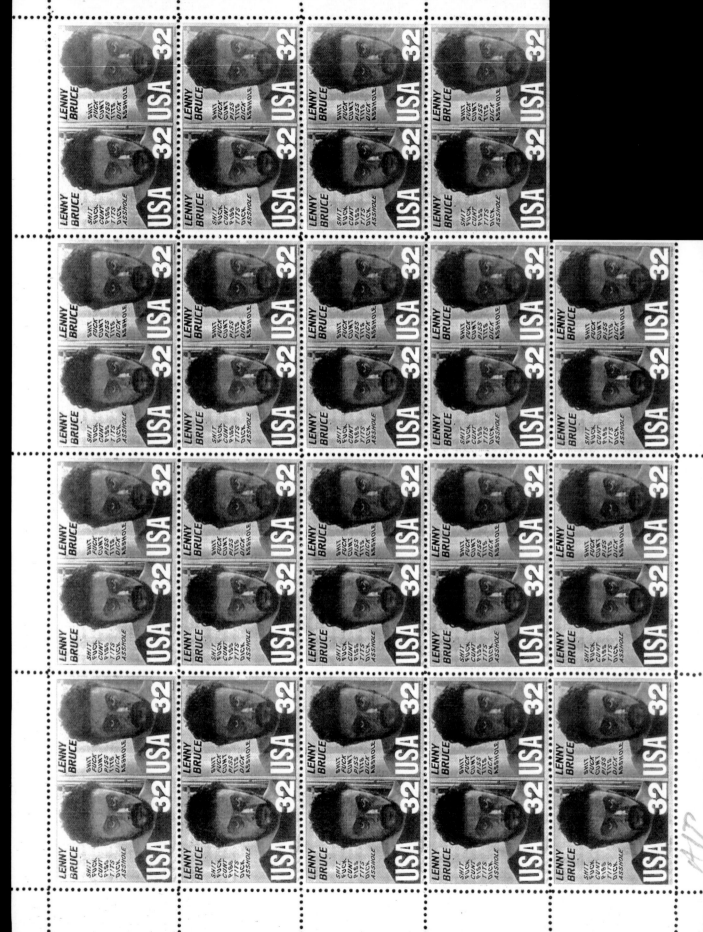

WASHINGTON, DC 200
PM
08 JAN
1999

OFFICE OF THE CLERK
SUPREME COURT OF THE UNITED STATES
WASHINGTON, DC 20543

OFFICIAL BUSINESS
PENALTY FOR PRIVATE USE $300

Mr. Daniel DeRuiter
40 Prospect S.E.
Grand Rapids, MI.
49503

49503-4318 30

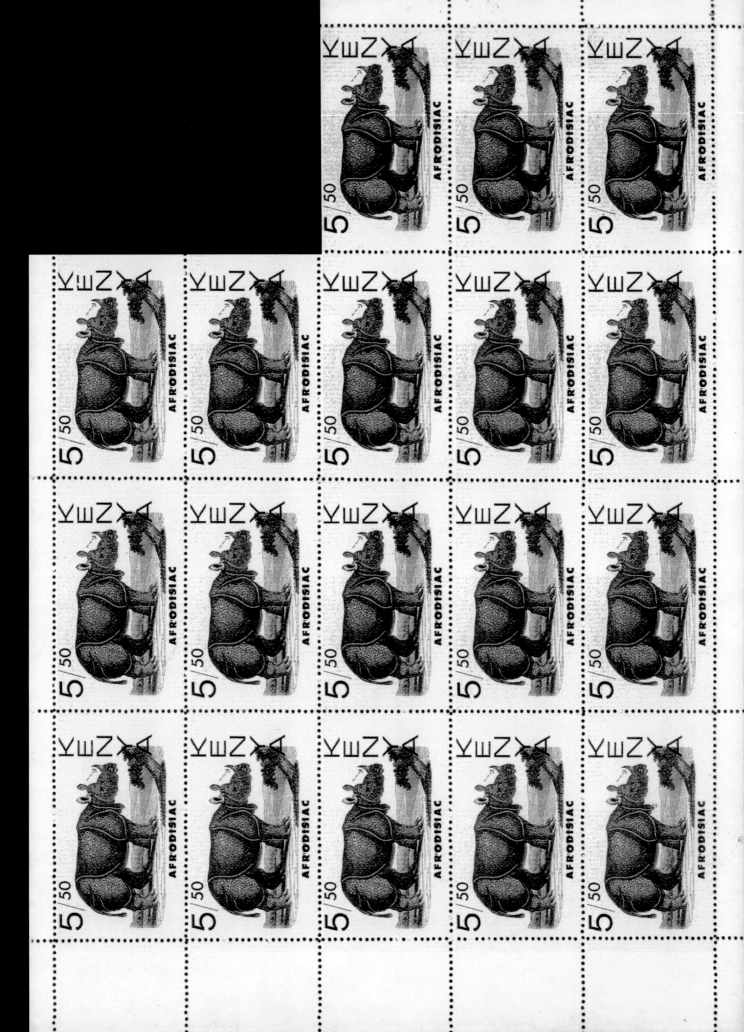

KENYA 5/50 AFRODISIAC

KENYA 5/50 AFRODISIAC

VIA AIR MAIL

Mr. Thompson
PO Box No. 12132
Chicago, Illinois
60612
USA

VIA AIR MAIL

60612/0132

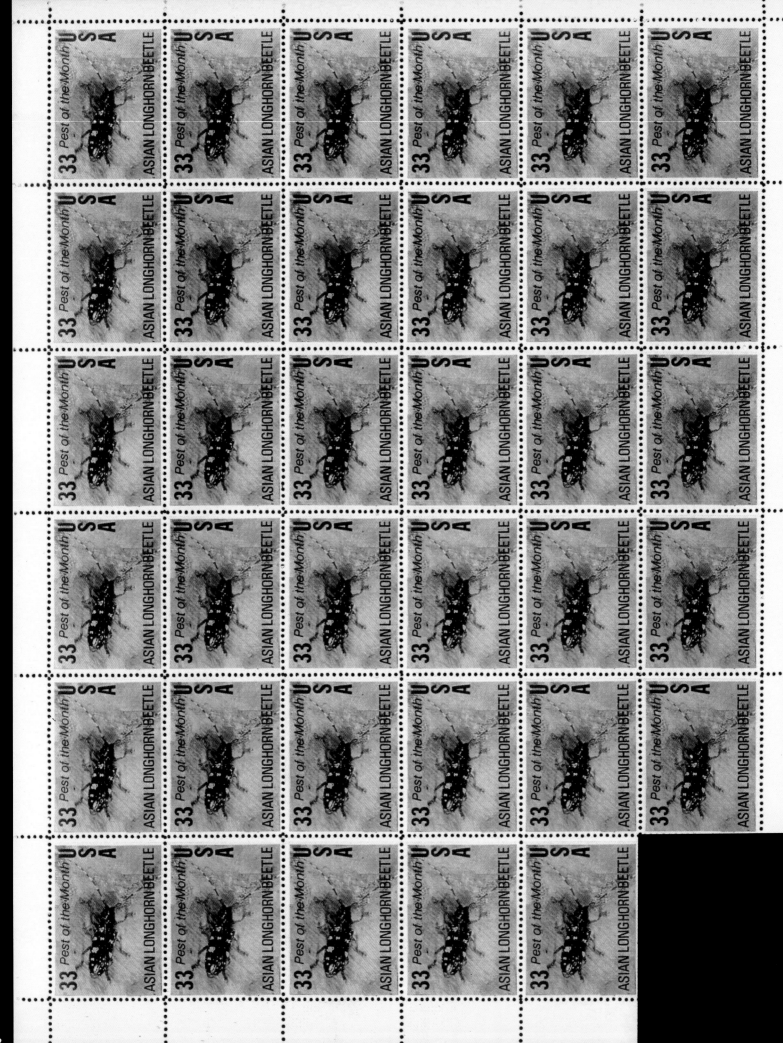

IRVING PARK ROAD PSDC IL
FEB 17 1999

Marilyn Ledner
330 W. 58th. St.
New York, NY   10019

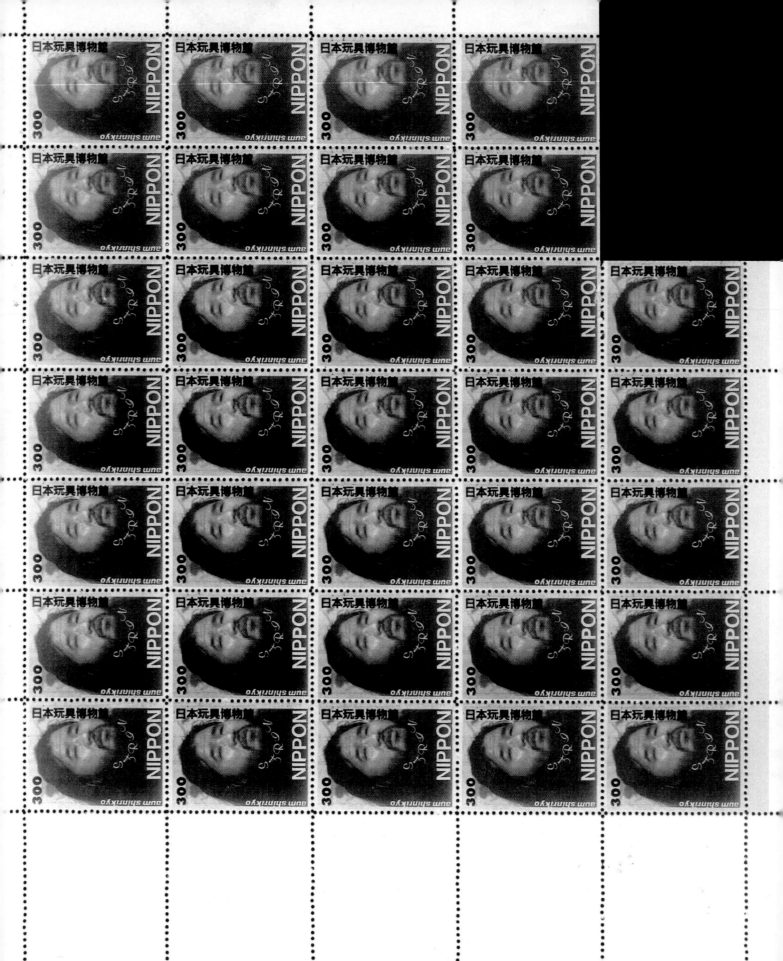

SERVICE DES POSTES 通信事務

日本玩具博物館 NIPPON 300 aum shinrikyo

日本玩具博物館 NIPPON 300 aum shinrikyo

Tokyo Central Post Office
Philatelic Section
CPO BOX 888, TOKYO 100-91 JAPAN

PAR AVION 航空郵便

Mr. Morlen Sinoway
2035 West Wabansia
Chicago, Illinois
60647

U/S/A

Printed Matter

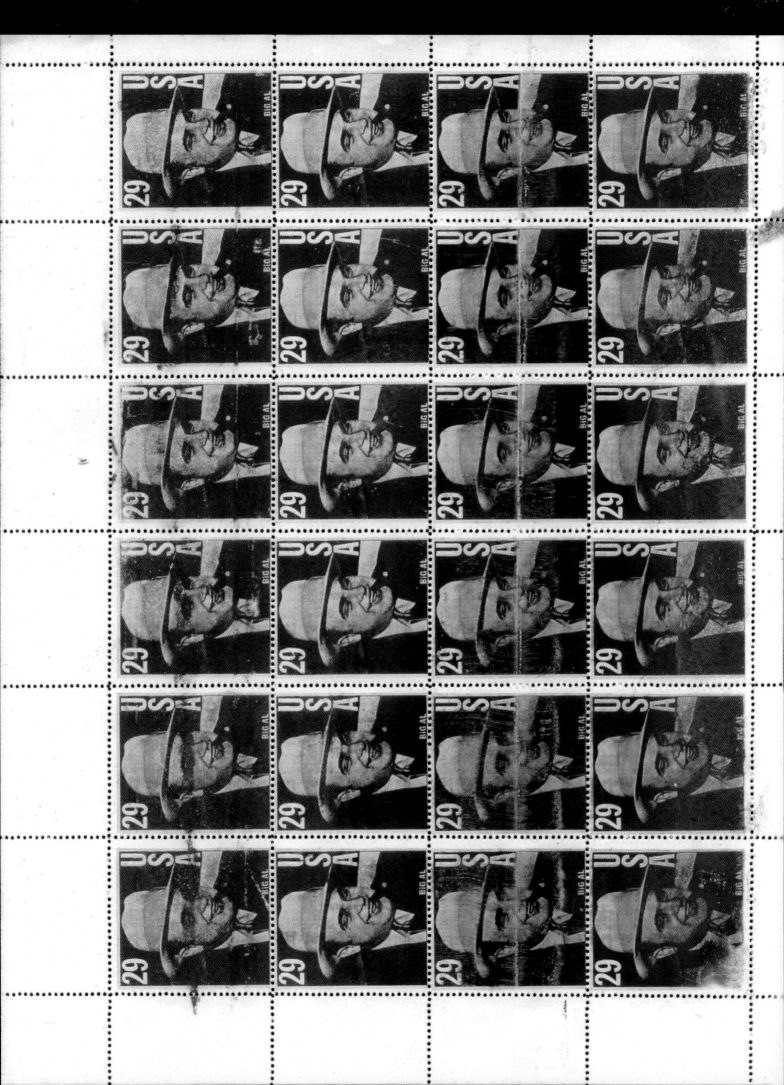

U S A
29

U S A
29

MICHAEL THOMPSON
PO BOX #106
500 WEST CERMAK RD
CHICAGO, IL. 60616

60616/1853

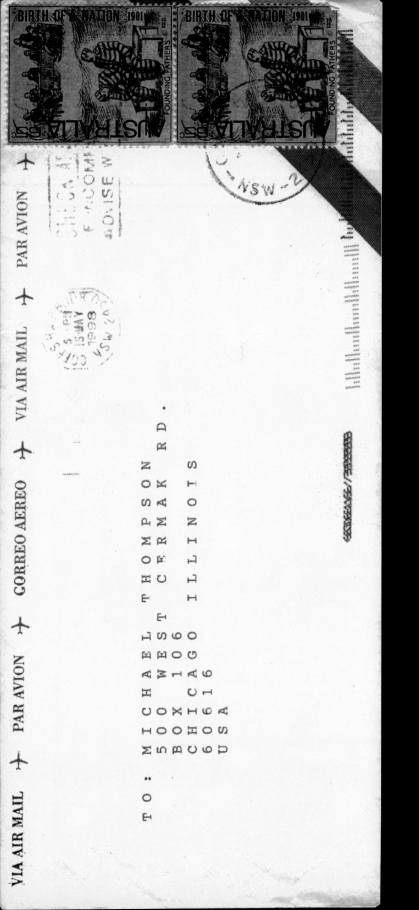

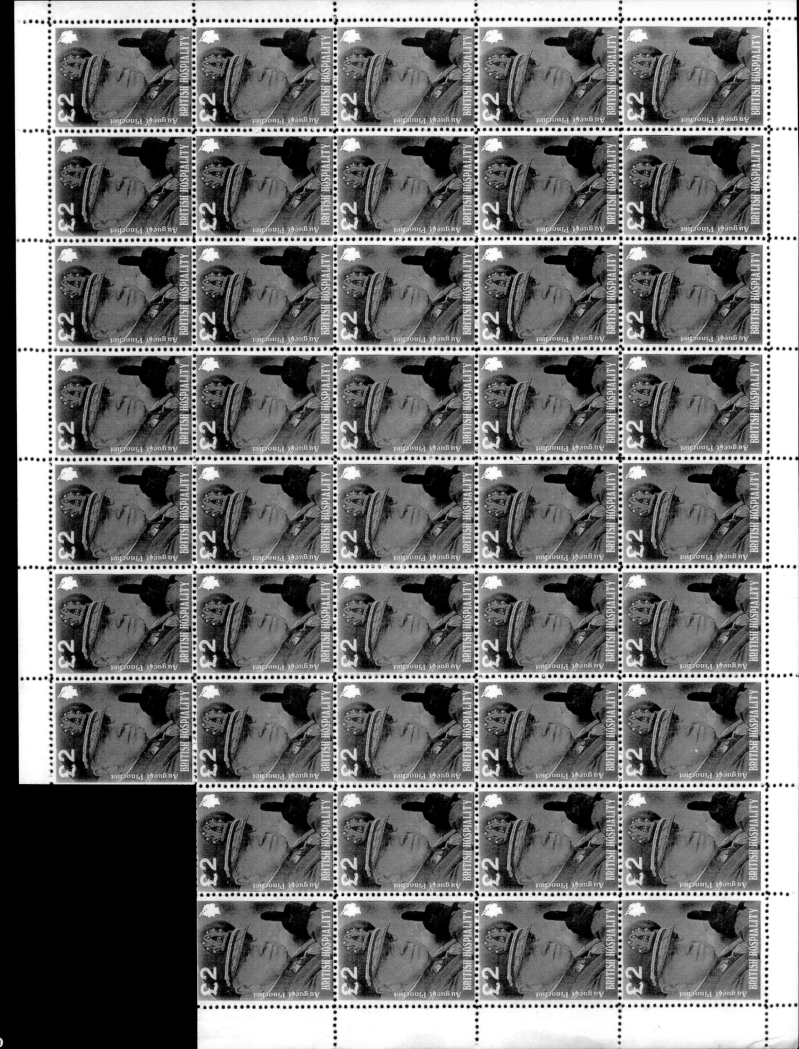

Disappear from . . .

. . . government agents, swat teams, seizures and privacy invaders . . . anyone you choose . . .

MS. FRANCE KOZLIK
798 SANTA BARBARA STREET
BERKELEY, CALIFORNIA
94702
U.S.A.

NORGE 8.00 CHERNOBYL-DEER
NORGE 8.00 CHERNOBYL DEER
NORGE 8.00 CHERNOBYL DEER
NORGE 8.00 CHERNOBYL DEER
NORGE 8.00 CHERNOBYL DEER

OWESEN & Co., A
STOCKHOLM · SWEDEN

Mr Raymond C Kapsted

Mrs. French Kozlick
798 Santa Barbara
Berkeley, California USA
94707

CHICAGO 50   Ill. USA

94707-2046 59

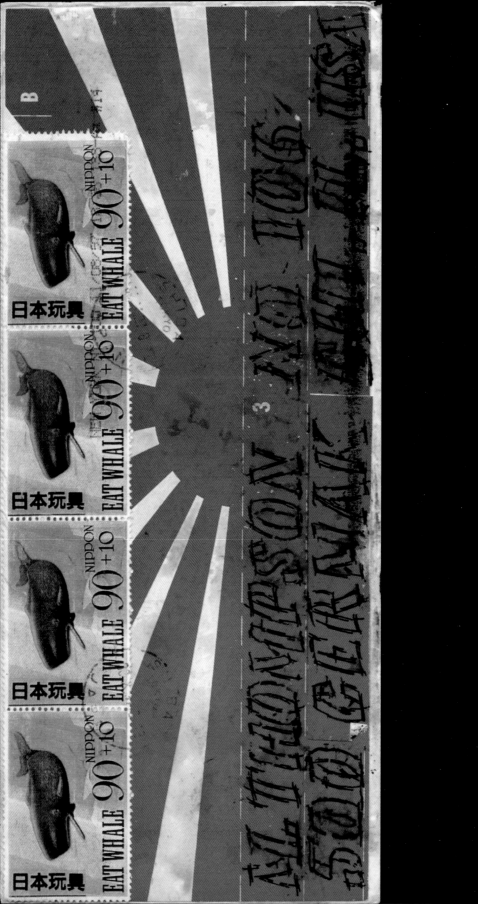

EAT WHALE — 1998 — Japanese cancellation

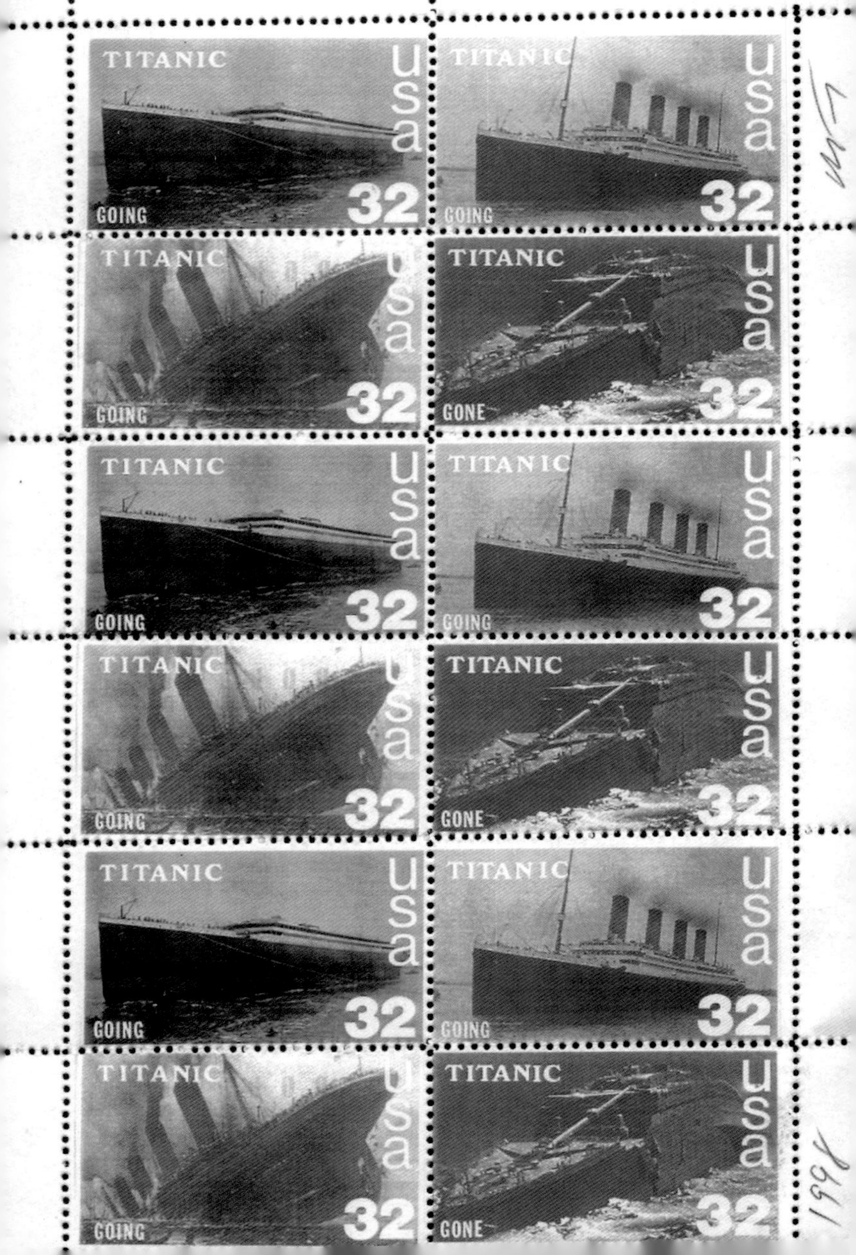

1998

USA 32 TITANIC GOING
USA 32 TITANIC GONE
USA 32 TITANIC GOING
USA 32 TITANIC GONE

GARY JUL 1998 PM 464

MT
DAN DERUITER
#1
40 PROSPECT S.E.
GRAND RAPIDS, MI. 49503

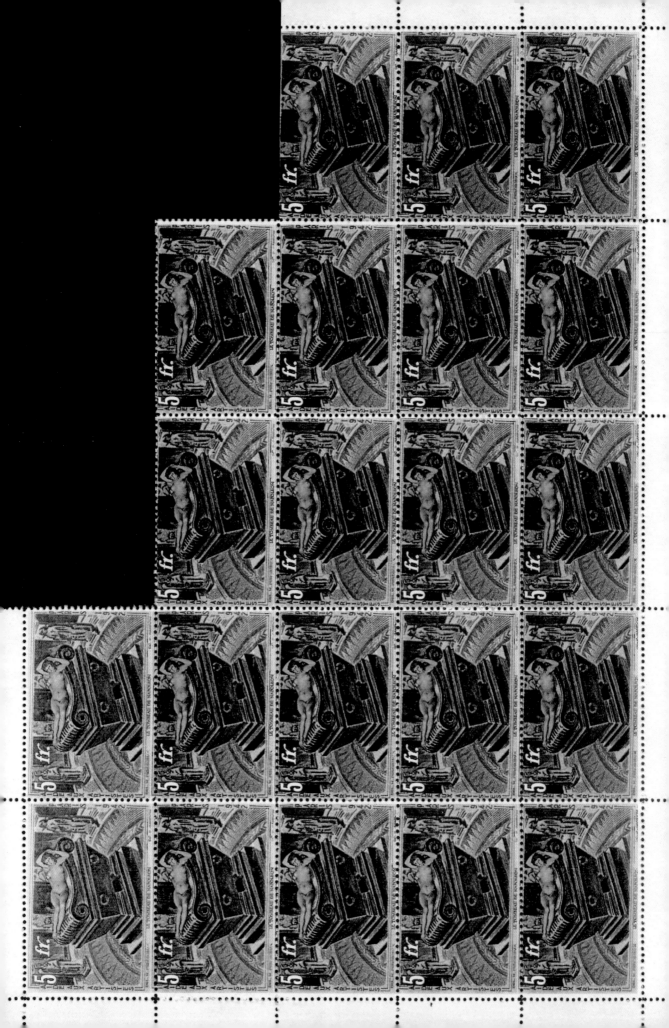

FILATURES & FILTERIES DE FRANCE
SIÈGE SOCIAL 3 ILLE 48 Rue de Valenciennes

Monsieur Sinoway
2035 West Wabansia
Chicago, Il'linois
60647   U.S.A.

ASCHAFFENBURG

VIA
AIRMAIL

VIA
AIRMAIL

VIA
AIRMAIL

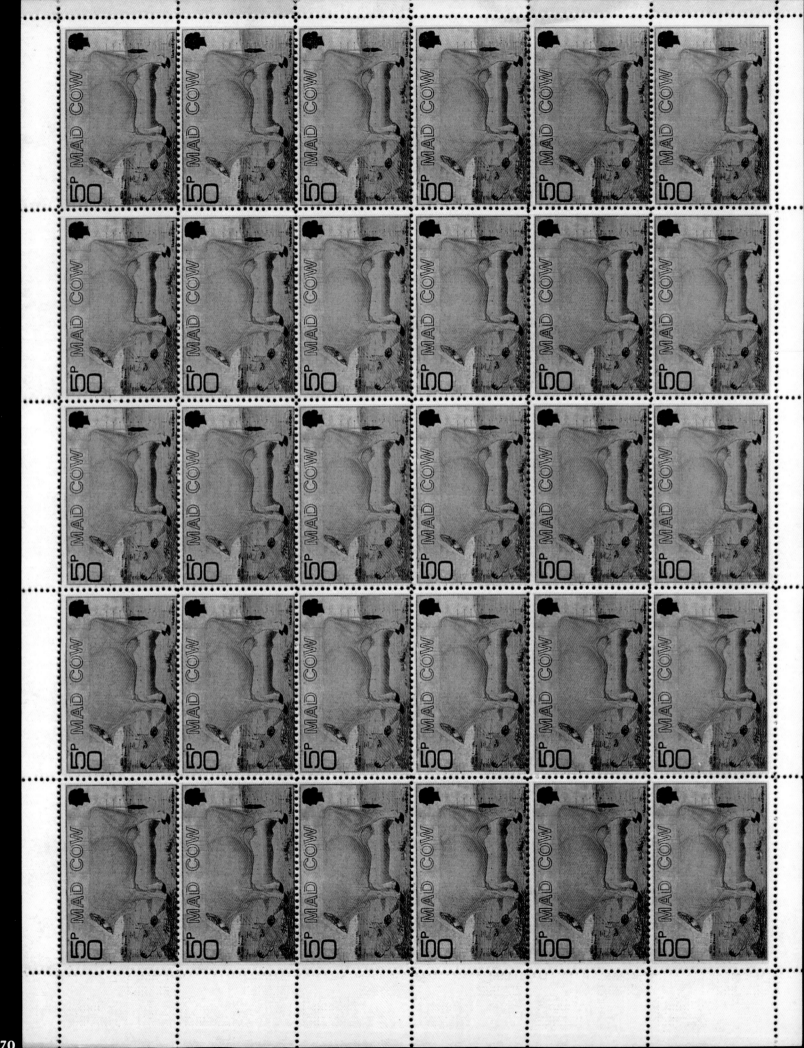

USA 32

BETTER RED THAN DEAD DAY

WASHINGTON, DC 200
PM
6 JAN
1997

OFFICE OF THE CLERK
SUPREME COURT OF THE UNITED STATES
WASHINGTON, DC 20543

OFFICIAL BUSINESS
PENALTY FOR PRIVATE USE $300

MR. MICHAEL F. THOMPSON
500 WEST CERMAK RD.
#106

CHICAGO, Il.   60616

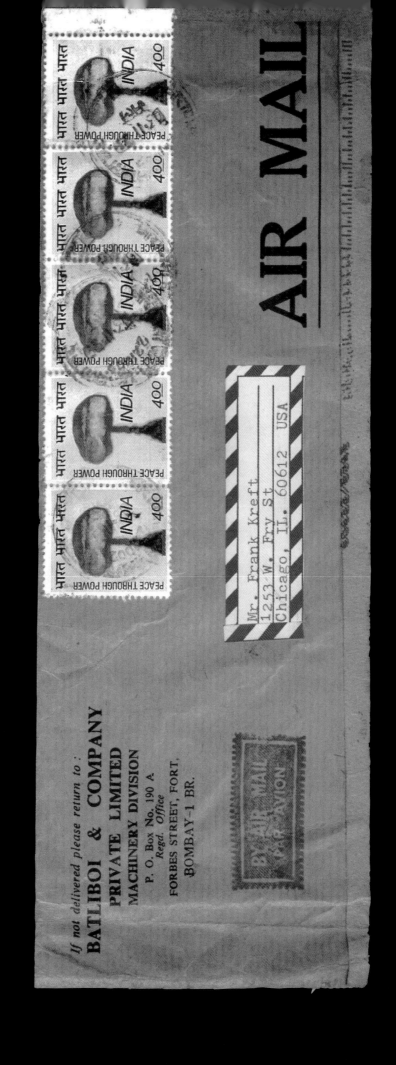

Peace Through Power — 1999 — Indian cancellation

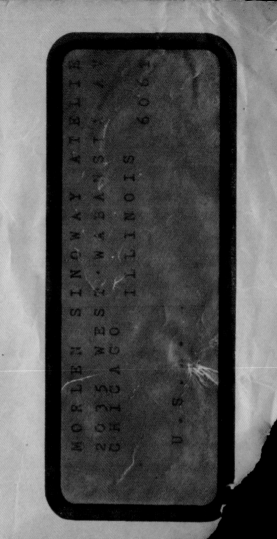

Schliemann (Schwindler und Pfuscher) — 1998 — German cancellation

USA 32 USA 32 USA 32
SEPARATE CHURCH AND STATE
USA 32 USA 32 USA 32 USA 32 USA 32 USA 32
SEPARATE CHURCH AND STATE SEPARATE CHURCH AND STATE
USA 32 USA 32 USA 32 USA 32 USA 32 USA 32
SEPARATE CHURCH AND STATE SEPARATE CHURCH AND STATE
USA 32 USA 32 USA 32 USA 32 USA 32 USA 32
SEPARATE CHURCH AND STATE SEPARATE CHURCH AND STATE
1/1 1997

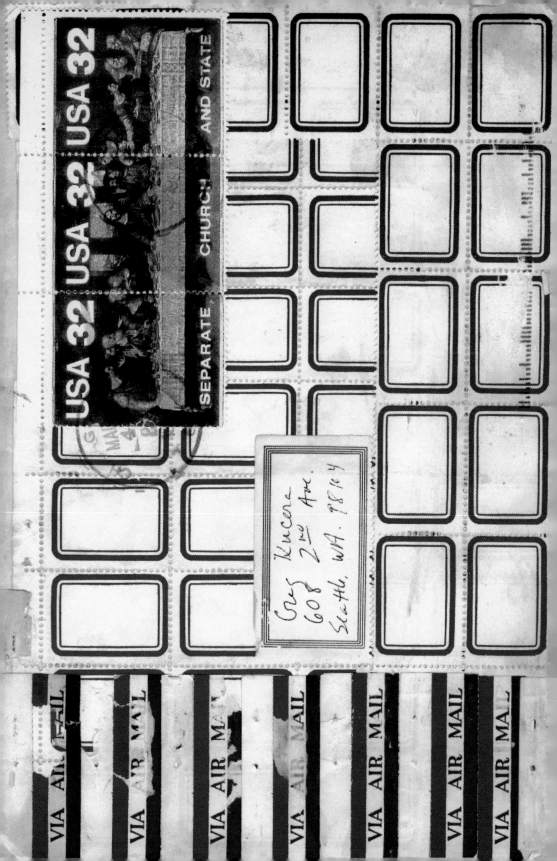

USA 32 USA 32 USA 32 USA 32

SEPARATE CHURCH AND STATE

Gus Kucera
608 2nd Ave.
Seattle, WA. 98104

VIA AIR MAIL VIA AIR MAIL VIA AIR MAIL VIA AIR MAIL VIA AIR MAIL VIA AIR MAIL VIA AIR MAIL

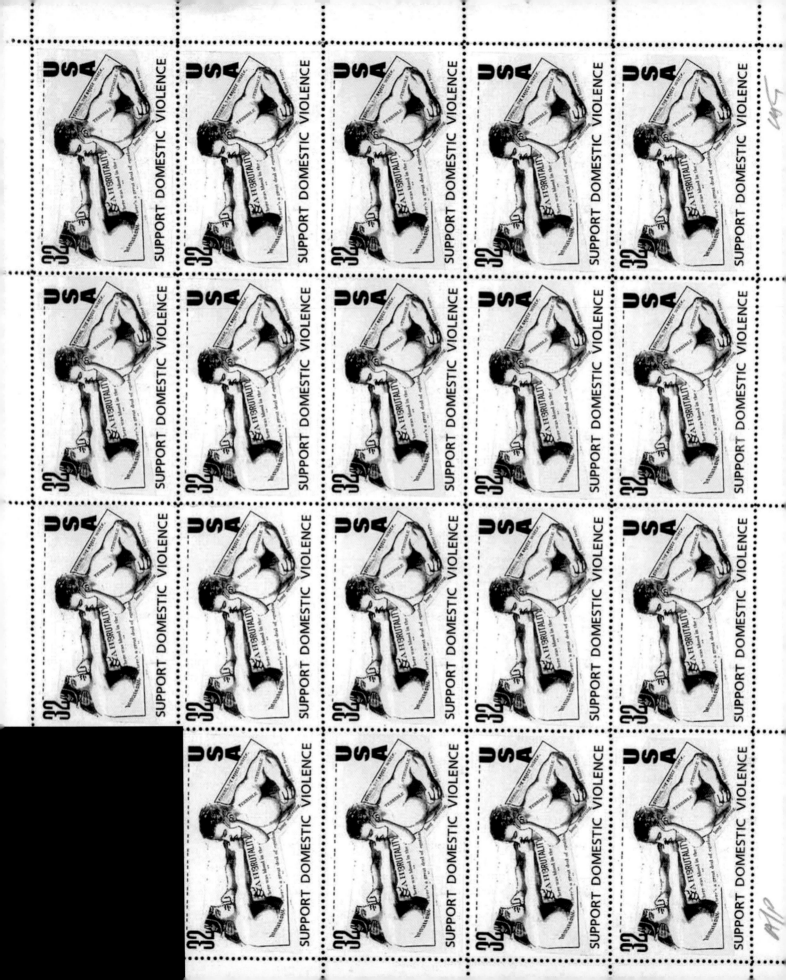

USA

SUPPORT DOMESTIC VIOLENCE

32

Thompson
Aron Packer
Suite 205
1579 Milaukee Ave
Chicago, Il. 60622

MERCHANDISE-
POSTMASTER: THI
FOR POSTAL INSP
RETURN POSTA

the necklace
R
S A
95c

SUID-AFRICA

the necklace
R
S A
95c

SUID-AFRICA

Republic of
South Africa
Republiek van
Suid-Afrika

Date-stamp card
Datumstempelkaart

PER LUGPOS
BY AIR MAIL
PAR AVION

Morlen Sinoway Atelier
2053 West Wabansia
2nd Floor

84

Alan Turner
10 Rathcoole Gardens
London N8 9NB   ENGLAND

The Stamp Art
and Postal History of

Michael Hernandez de Luna

The Stamp Story
By Michael Hernandez de Luna, Chicago, Illinois

I suppose my involvement with stamps began in Iowa City in 1987, when I purchased vintage USA stamps from the '50s through '70s, simply for the purpose of decorating envelopes. The stamps were a variety of commemoratives showing famous battle scenes from the Civil War, various dead presidents, images of Boy Scouts — all total Americana. The stamps interested me because they added philatelic color to envelopes I was posting. What made this really interesting was the need to use a lot of stamps, as a result of the very low stamp denominations, just pennies for the most part. Normal postage back then was around 25 cents. At the time, I was totally unaware that I was starting my first adventure into mail art and philately.

While I was living in Germany from 1988 through 1994, my interest in collecting stamps grew stronger, partly because I thought this could be a fruitful way of meeting women: "Hey baby, you wanna come up and see my stamp collection?" It never worked. I found myself browsing the windows of stamp and coin shops. I bought two sets of postage stamps which caught my eye because of the artwork. The first set was a collection from Vietnam, Laos and Cambodia from the mid through late '80s which featured a variety of reptiles, mainly snakes. They were very large as far as stamp size goes, and a very beautiful series. The other set was sport stamps from Russia's 1980 Olympics series. The stamps were designed in a Greek art style: figurative, classical and statuesque. The stamps themselves are quite striking, with the central image printed in duotone within a vignette of contrasting color. Little did I know that these three stamp acquisitions would lead me to this point in stamp designing and put me in the ranks with Senator Dan Rostenkowski and Ted Kaczynski, both very well-known for mail crimes of different natures.

In 1994 I returned to Chicago, bought a 1976 Postal Jeep and began making fake stamps. At that time I found that Michael Thompson had been working on a stamp project for several years, making what I call his mono stamps, which are one-of-a-kind fake stamps. He invited me to enter the picture, so naturally I did. Since my background involves the knowledge of printmaking, some computer skills, and influences of Pop sensibilities, I began thinking about the postage stamp sheet and presentation of the work. I introduced the idea of sheets and it was welcomed. It seemed natural to present the envelope and sheet side-by-side at exhibitions. The printmaking issues raised by the work were very interesting on account of the situation that naturally occurred when removing a single stamp from the sheet and affixing it to an envelope. These issues created a conflict in the rules of printmaking. On the one hand, there is the very formal stamp sheet, dealing with the edition element of sameness. In editions, this is the numbering of each image printed from the printing plate or stone. This is always marked in a fraction: 10/56, for example, which means it is the tenth print made out of 56. On the other hand, the conflict created by the stamp's removal from the sheet is that it becomes an element to decorate the postal envelope and no longer a part of the sameness aspect of the sheet from which it was removed. The issues raised become a melting pot of conceptual ideas: subversive, anarchistic, and anti-edition. The printmaking process is expanded to include the postal system and its method of canceling or marking the envelopes. The print or stamp which belonged to the sheet of stamps becomes an integrated element of the envelope with its new markings.

While researching the fake postage stamp history, I stumbled onto some names important to the Stamp Project. One is Spanish Surrealist José Argemi, who designed artist stamps, during the heyday of Surrealism, though the

exact dates of his production of art stamps are unknown to me. I have no idea if they were ever actually used as stamps. I can only assume, given the nature of the Surrealist subconscious twisting of reality that someone could have explored this notion, unnoticed and undocumented. In the early '90s, I purchased several reissued stamp sheets by Robert Watts, an American Fluxus artist who many say was responsible for the fake postage stamp idea as its known today: artistamps, or artist stamps, as I like to refer to them. Prior to Watts was the French New Realist artist, Yves Klein, whose monochrome blue stamp I consider the first modern or contemporary functional artist stamp. Watts followed in the '60s; his ideas and work are a great influence on many of us who create fake postage stamps. But let's keep in mind the importance of the conceptual aspects of Klein's blue stamp: he created a solid-color stamp (the blue stamp), placed it on a solid white envelope, and sent it through the mail. The stamp is comparable to Russian artist Kasimir Malevich's 1920s Supremacist paintings of a square of color within a square of color, which might even be considered the genesis of the blue stamp.

I see the art of painting a canvas transformed in size and concept in Klein's stamp. The philatelic object created, the stamp, is affixed to the envelope for it's journey and collection of markings. The envelope is personalized by addressing it with a recipient's name. It is then tagged with the fake stamp for the the action of being dropped into a mailbox. The stamp goes on an unknown journey down a labyrinth of conveyor belts before reaching its' journeys destination. The blue stamp gave that common journey a new twist. It created the element of chance. It's what I call the "mortality factor," an element in the journey that silently plagues this project. The mortality factor occurs when the envelope with the stamp is confiscated, lost, or (I'd like to believe) stolen by a cohort accomplice. Klein's exploit becomes more than just his artwork. It becomes a performance in a functional, transient, anarchic bundle of concepts and ideas beyond the boundaries of modern art of the period. It becomes philatelic.

Klein designed only one stamp which I know of, the blue stamp, which was used to mail out his exhibition invitations. It's been documented that Klein sent out 3500 invitations. In 1957 this was revolutionary and actually unheard of in philately, as well as in the art world of the period. Klein has been documented mailing his blue stamp from 1957 through 1959. The conceptual theory behind this action goes beyond a modern painting or a sculpture of the time: it becomes entertainment through the media or public outrage. We see now that Yves Klein's documented conceptual prank opened up new approaches which advanced the elements of printmaking, performance, collage, chance, and conceptual art simultaneously, all through his action of creating a stamp, affixing it to an envelope and putting it in the mail. I hope this is one way in which the stamps and envelopes in this book will be perceived.

I want to revive the issues raised by Klein's blue stamp: they seem to have gotten lost by the wayside, no longer noticed by the world from which they came and unnoticed by philately. However, noted or not, the concept has survived through the four succeeding decades. Going back to '50s philatelic history, the concept of a flat plane or shape as a stamp, commemorating a color, surely would have rattled the stamp world then, as it certainly would now.

I don't consider myself a philatelic expert, or even a philatelist, even though my passion is collecting old envelopes and giving them a new vitality by adding my own creations. One of the elements which gives new life to these old envelopes is the authentification of new postal cancellation marks. This is achieved by resending these reworked envelopes through the postal stream. Since my main objective is to design stamps for use, it's my belief that I stay true to philately by using the materials of this hobby. The envelope becomes my canvas and glue sticks, air mail stickers, rubber stampers, stencils, labels and other such items become my tools. Mail art, the blue stamp, and this stamp project wouldn't exist without the function of the postal system or philately. The solicited collaboration of phantom postal employees, machines and the journey is the project's process which gives credibility to the work. As an artist working in the field of stamp designing, I think one needs to understand philately. I find knowledge of the field rewarding while creating these stamps. The end result — the canceled stamp — always brings on a mischievous smile.

In 1970 the American artist Ray Johnson coined the phrase "Mail Art" for a growing army of artists who were joining the ranks of sending art through the post. This became the network of mail artists who hail Johnson as the Godfather of mail art, like James Brown is to funk music. Johnson worked from the late '50s through the early '90s, weaving in and out of the Pop and Fluxus channels and becoming a mail art icon with his New York Correspondence School, which furthered the idea of mailing art as communication. Johnson's art was about correspondence. He included many of the players (artists) of the time in his game of sending art camouflaged as mail back and forth through the post. He was, in my opinion, an artists' artist. The work was free, liberating, and functioned outside the smugness of the art world of the time. I think the amazing element of Johnson's work is the physical act of mailing, be it letters, post cards or objects. It becomes a game of mailing art, and games between two persons frequently turn into relationships of sorts. I use the word "game" because every so often things which get sent through the post become the challenge and set up for competition. For example, one day I send you an old shoe. So, you raise the ante and send me a fisherman's boot, covered with pages of that Hemingway novel, *For Whom the Bell Tolls* glued all over it like a piñata. This is the magic of Johnson's work, and this is the way I want the work in this book to function: the idea of a game, each stamp competing with the previous, kind of like Mad magazine's *Spy vs. Spy*, or me vs. Thompson. So this new art form has turned into a postal game which I call PRANKSTERHOOD. I suppose if I had to give the game a proper name it could be called the New U.S. Service's Citizens' Advisory Committee of MHDL.

I began collecting an archive of images when I was in art school, and have continued the practice. I found that my first body of ideas for the fake stamps was complete in 1994. In the beginning, the ideas were all over the place. Nevertheless, they worked. I had tapped into something that just took off on its own, and it was entertaining. Like Thompson, I was hooked. My very first stamps were a set of Kama Sutras, USA issue. There were about seven stamps on the sheet, depicting different sex positions and reflecting the concept that sex plus religion equals a smile. My next set of stamps, also USA issue, were the breast stamps, a very big hit with both sexes. This was a sheet of 36 sets of different pairs of breasts. I included the names of past girlfriends to pay homage to the lovely pears (fruits) they had. What followed next was an array of images: comics, dead people, murders, condoms, nudes, politicians gone bad, drugs, religion, genitalia, etc. A bit outrageous and shocking by normal standards, however, the work had political overtones, reflecting social commentary and popular culture with the subversive edge of a sharp knife. Sometimes it feels like you could be viewing the work through the bottom of a whiskey glass.

Courtesy of the Artist

My first side show exhibition — and first real audience — was in 1994, in a bar where I used to hang out. I had an appreciative audience who acknowledged their enjoyment by buying me beers in trade for stamps, or on occasion buying stamps for cash. This experience had definite Fluxus overtones: spontaneous, unpredictable and fun.

All the while, the envelopes went out and came back, pouring into my mail box. I remember December 29, 1994 distinctly because it was quite an amazing postal day. The postman delivered 13 different breast envelopes, among many others which I can't recall this moment. My hands were filled with my highly-prized junk mail; I was laughing to myself with a sense I was being watched. In 1996 it became apparent that the more mail I sent out, the less

I received in return. It was the mortality factor silently pillaging the work. I would send out dozens of envelopes into the mail stream, with sometimes a zero return ratio. This was putting stress on the vein power, if you know what I mean. Well, a slight case of paranoia set in. The work output for that year was meager. Then, in 1997, I was contacted by the Seattle Postal Inspectors. The first "cease and desist" letter arrived, and summarized it read: "A possible violation of Federal law which you appear to be associated with has come to the attention of this office." The interesting point of this letter: it made reference to the matter of me instigating or initiating an idea which was illegal and for which I could be penalized. It was this *Fahrenheit 451* freedom mentality control. My lawyer and I ignored the order. But they were nice enough to return several envelopes along with the letter. The one you can view in this book is called Jesus was just a Man, and Mary was just a Woman / Love 2...

Months later another letter arrived, with a milder tone toward me and a change of psychology. It was going after the gallery's involvement with me, which resulted in the gallery postponing an exhibition which had been planned for quite a while, before kindly dumping the exhibition entirely, along with me and Mr. Thompson.

The interesting point in both letters was that they would deliver my mail, but "postage due." This is an exact quote from the second letter: "Any further mailings with this fraudulent postage will be delivered to you postage due." That was ok with me. I asked my gallery people to pay the postage and collect receipts. It's not my intention to deprive the postal service of any revenue. I see it as using the printmaking services which are available through this governmental tributary. It's about the system's involvement with the process of creating the work through the collaboration of the phantom cohorts: machines and clerks. I'm fine with the concept of postage due. I'll pay it. It's only proper for me to pay, since I am using a bureaucratic institution to make my art. It's a nice safeguard the postal service has in place.

One gallery exhibiting my work actually paid the postman. He had gone so far as to note on the envelope that this was not a real stamp, and funds were required to receive it. He hand-delivered the envelope and note to the director of the gallery, who read the note and paid the man. Unfortunately, the gallery forgot to get a receipt. Nevertheless, I framed the two notes: the envelope from the postman along with the gallery director's account of the story. Throughout the stamp project's history, letters from mysterious postal persons questioning the validity of the stamps have occurred on occasion. These letters or notes sometimes arrive within official U.S. Postal envelopes including the fake stamped envelope. Other times the envelope arrives with notes scribbled on its' surface or, in rare cases, body bags. Body bags are official clear plastic envelopes that the postal service uses to return damaged goods.

The work attracts me because the span of the ideas and concepts of 20th century art history that fall under the project's umbrella. Since the work is based on appropriation and satire, my appropriation theory functions through parody and satirizing the original image's meaning and idea through recycling and reinventing. The work has this natural characteristic of recycling and reinventing itself, similar to musicians working with sound sampling and tape looping. Creating images which already exist is not necessary for the art of designing stamps. During the course of a day, a person is bombarded with thousands of images through broadcast media, periodicals, and other publications. Out of all those images which one subconsciously witnesses throughout the day, recall of them is close to zero. This work is all about commemorating Pop culture with these passing images.

As an artist, I search for the best image possible to exploit and mirror popular culture through stamp designing. I look through an array of magazines both new and old, collecting pictures and ideas rated "G" through "X." Basically, I find images that connect with me. So, I tweak or hot-rod them, set a stamp denomination with press type, and send them on their journey through the mail. Maybe it was my Marcel Duchamp alter ego who said "All art is recycled and reinvented."

By February of 1998 my designing and stamp sending output was back to normal. The mortality factor silently consumed my highly prized junk mail. Postal delivery numbers were low, but nevertheless, they were arriving.

I was planning an exhibition of new work at a Chicago gallery. The weather had been unusually mild for that time of the year. The first storm that rolled in was one of an entirely different nature, armed complete with badges, guns, and business cards from the Chicago Postal Investigation Department. The Postal Inspectors came, saw, and warned us to cease and desist. Michael Thompson had the singular pleasure of speaking with them face to face. After trying to catch me off guard at home, they called to set up an appointment. Having been fully warned about the preceding chain of events and what was to come, I was prepared. So when they phoned me several days after their visit to Thompson, I declined their invitation and referred the matter to my attorney. I received the official cease and desist order by certified post on the day of our exhibition, February 13, 1998. Naturally, I framed it. It was my best piece in the show.

The exhibition went off without any glitches, meaning no one went to jail. Michael and I bickered for a while about who was number one on the Postal Inspectors' case list. It turned out we tied: we're listed under the same case number: **380-120-1365 RI (1).** We figure the Postal Inspectors are our biggest collectors to date.

The following pages of my work are some of the envelopes which survived the Mortality Factor. ∎

JUST HORSEN AROUND
DOGGY STYLE

32

MINUTES OF FUN

Santa Fe, N·M

Hernandez de Luna / Aron Packer Gallery
1579 N. Milwaukee / **Room 205** CHGO. IL 60622

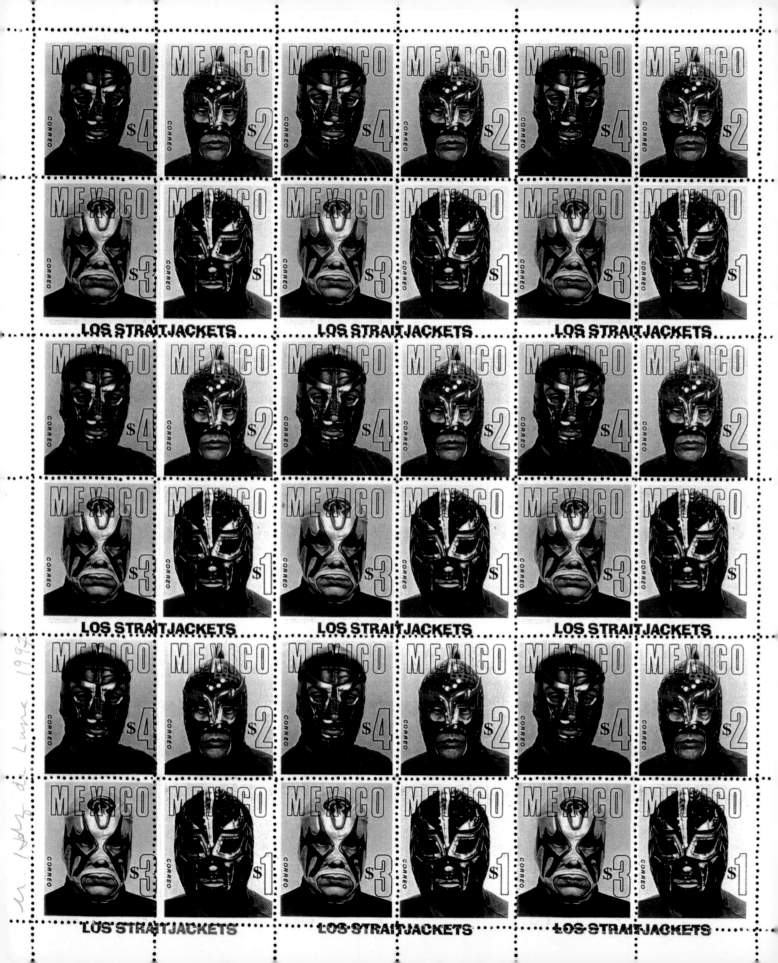

MHDL

PO...

Umberto Rucco

3612

400 N McClurg

CHGO IL 60611

USA

MEXICO

$3

LOS STRAI

PAR AVION
AIR MAIL
CORREO AEREO
PAR AVION

Los Straightjackets — 1997 — Mexican cancellation

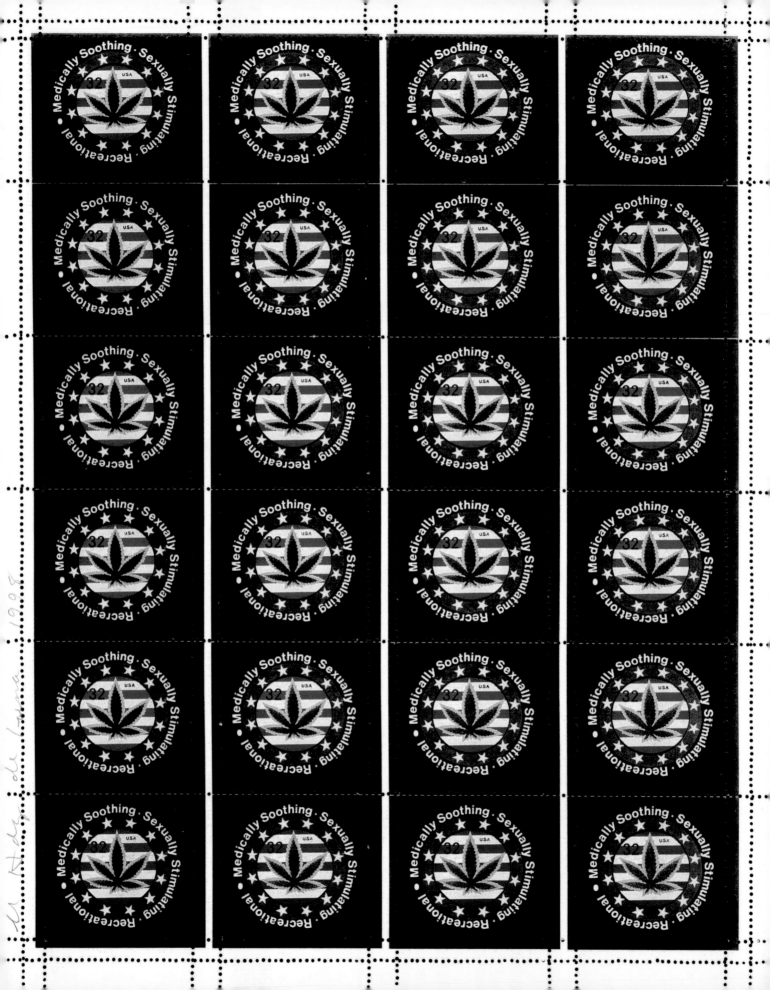

MINISTÉRIO DA AGRICULTURA

Medically Soothing · Sexually Stimulating · Recreational · USA

AIR MAIL
Fly Capital Airlines Constellations

PALATINE
DEC 13
1998
PM
60095

Illinois

U.S.A.

M. SEYL
c/o M. H. D. L.
Lenau Str. 49
60318 Frankfurt
G E R M A N Y

BELO HORIZONTE

0014970000

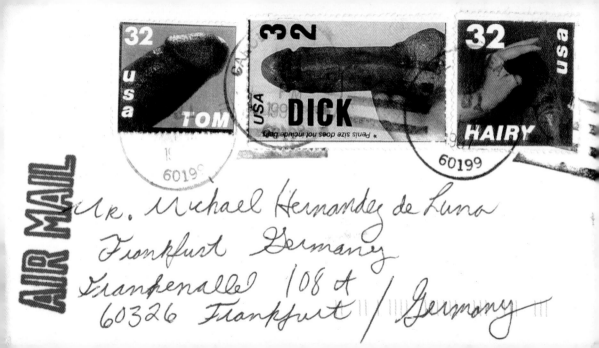

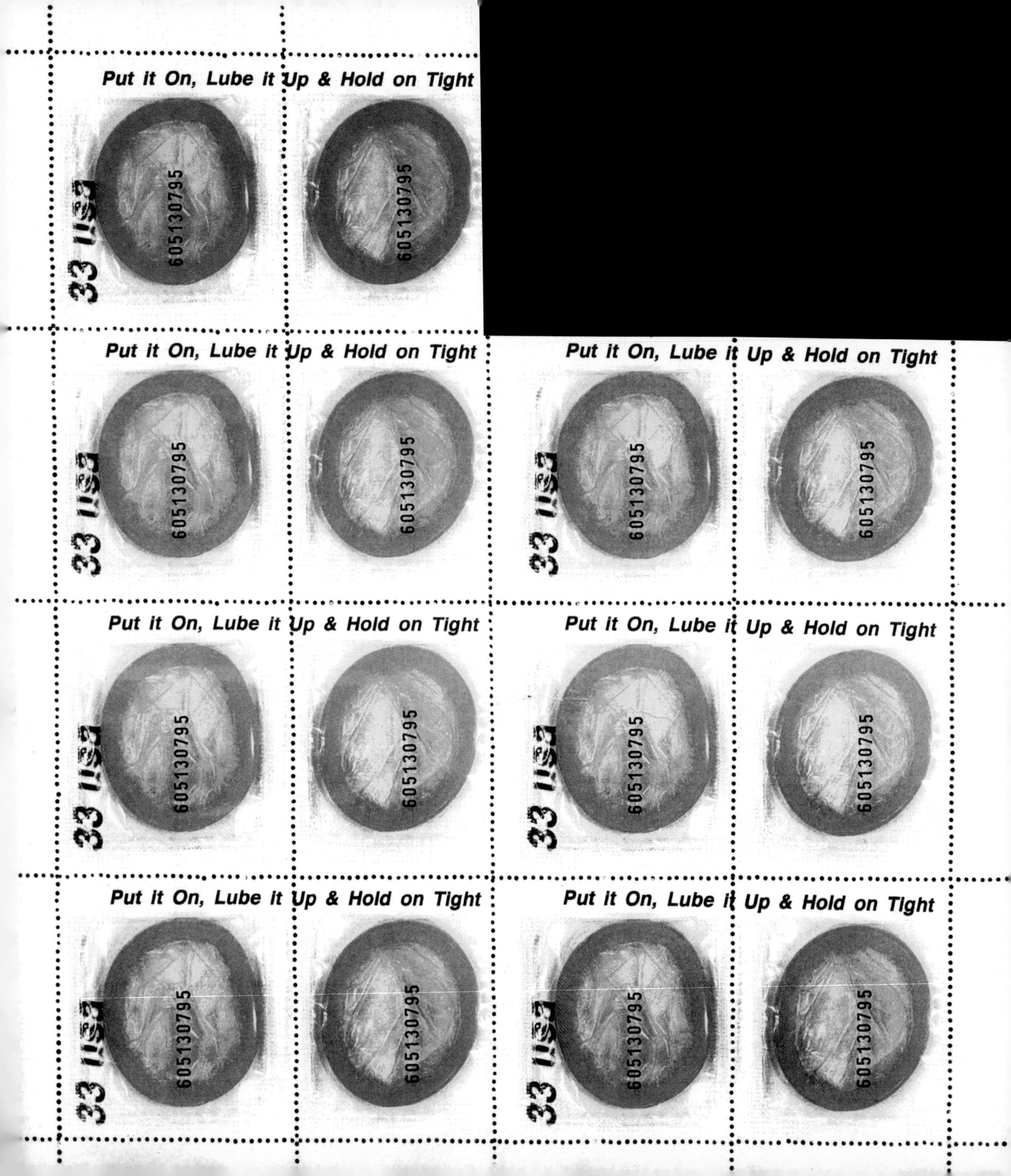

AUTHORISED SOUVENIR COVER

Put it On, Lube it Up & Hold on Tight

Buy
HEALTH STAMPS
for
**CHILDREN'S HEALTH
CAMPS**

CHILDREN'S HEALTH
IS THE
NATION'S WEALTH.

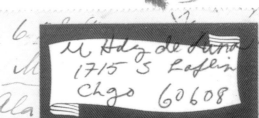

M Hdz de Luna
1715 S Loflin
Chgo 60608

El B. J. — 1992 — Mexican cancellation

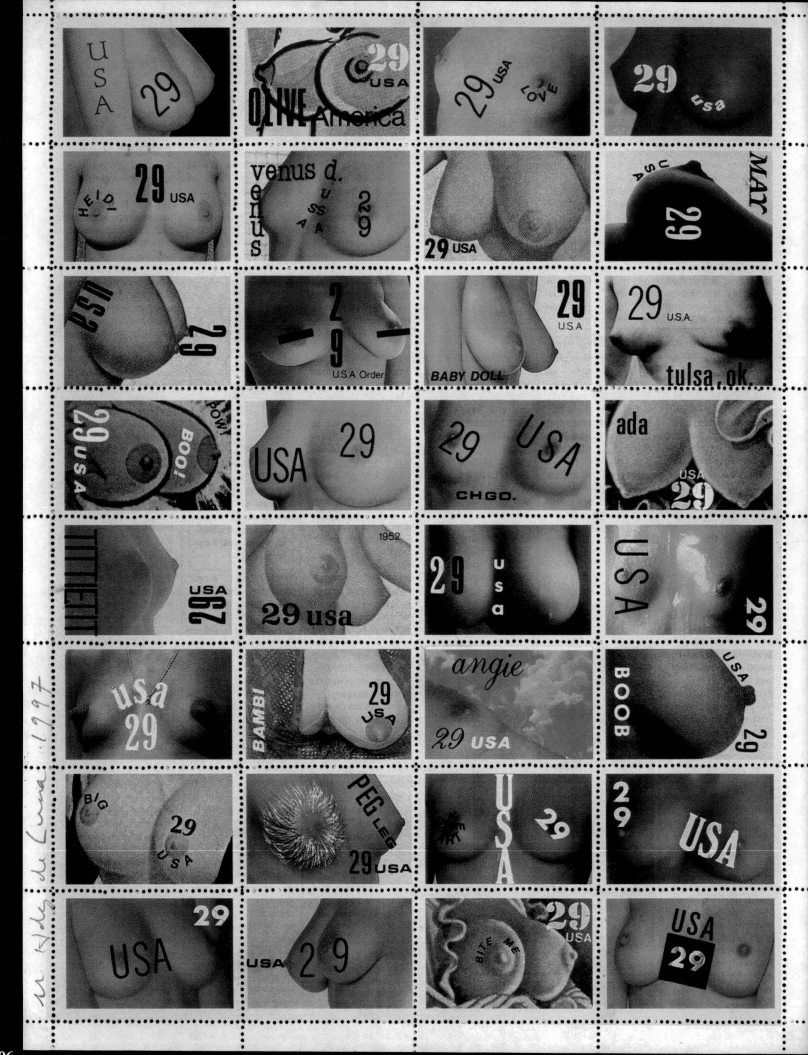

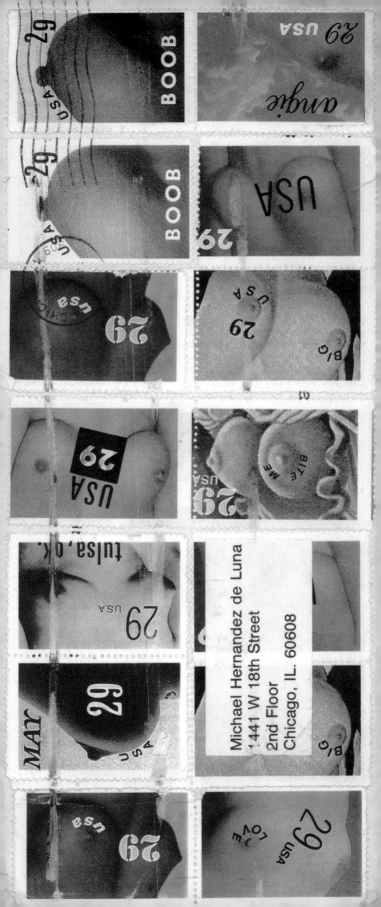

Michael Hernandez de Luna
1441 W 18th Street
2nd Floor
Chicago, IL. 60608

FOUND LOOSE IN THE MAILS

US 32 C

SIN NER

Michael Hernandez de Luna 1441 West 18th Street Chgo, IL 60608

UNITED STATES POSTAL SERVICE
CHICAGO CENTRAL FACILITY
NIXIE SECTION - TOUR
CHICAGO, ILLINOIS 60607

1171

PM

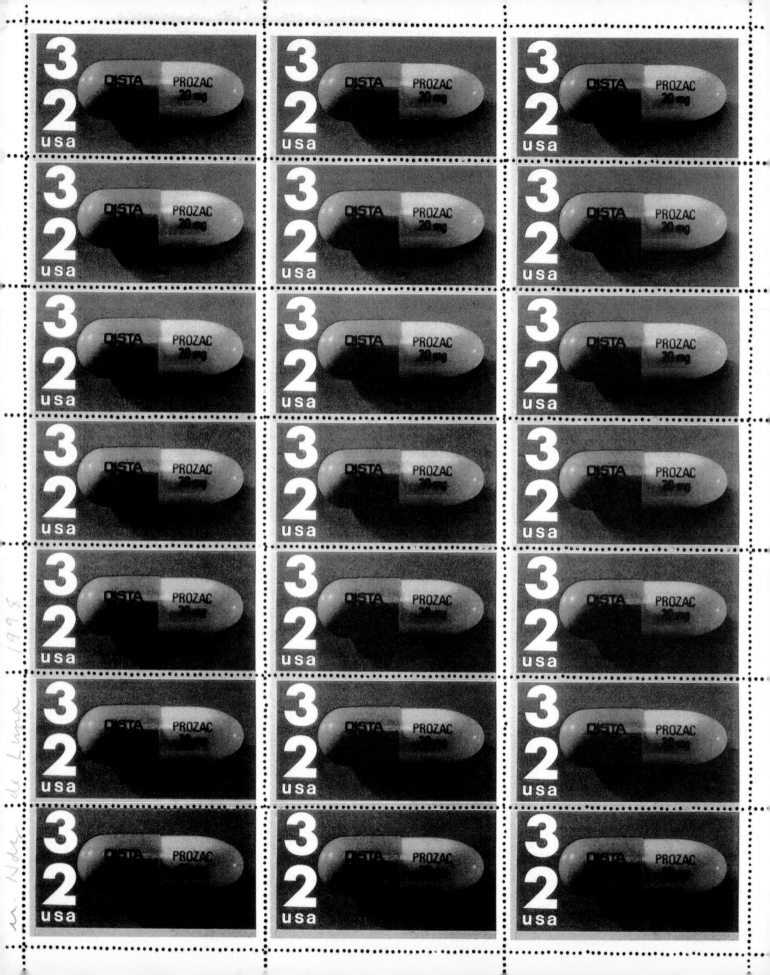

MHDL 1715 South Laflin Chgo IL 60608

Michael Hernandez de Luna.

HERNANDEZ : S. Cummins Gallery 12 Miller Ave. MILL VALLEY, CA. 94941 St.

Chicago, IL 60608.

60608/3035 41

c — 1998

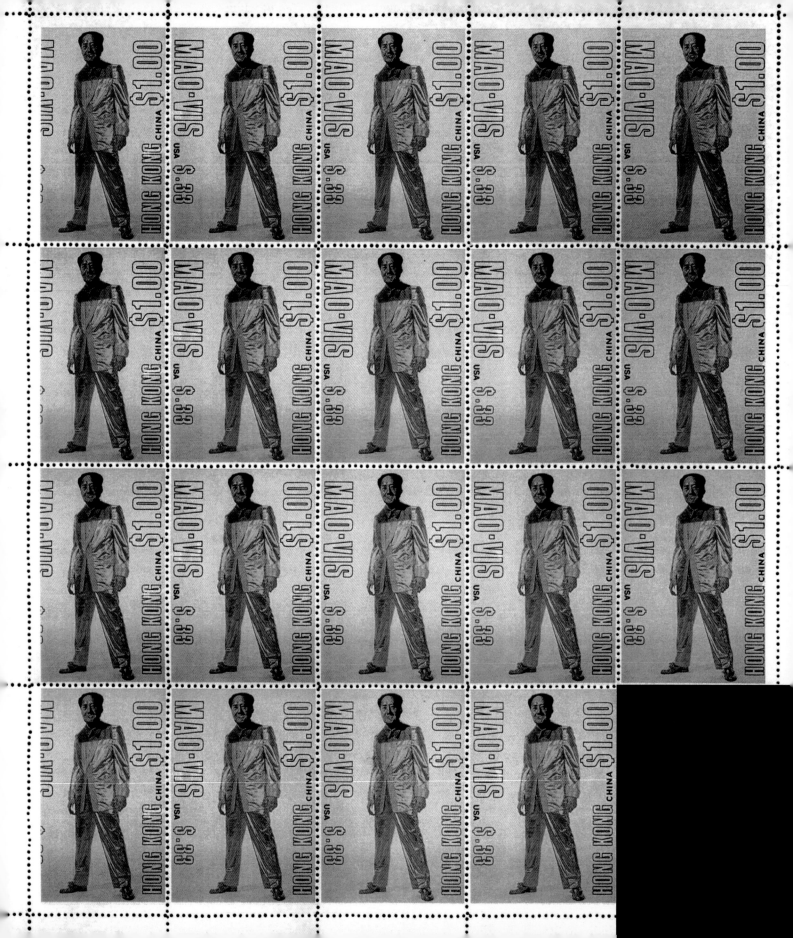

MAO-VIS — 1999 — Hong Kong cancellation

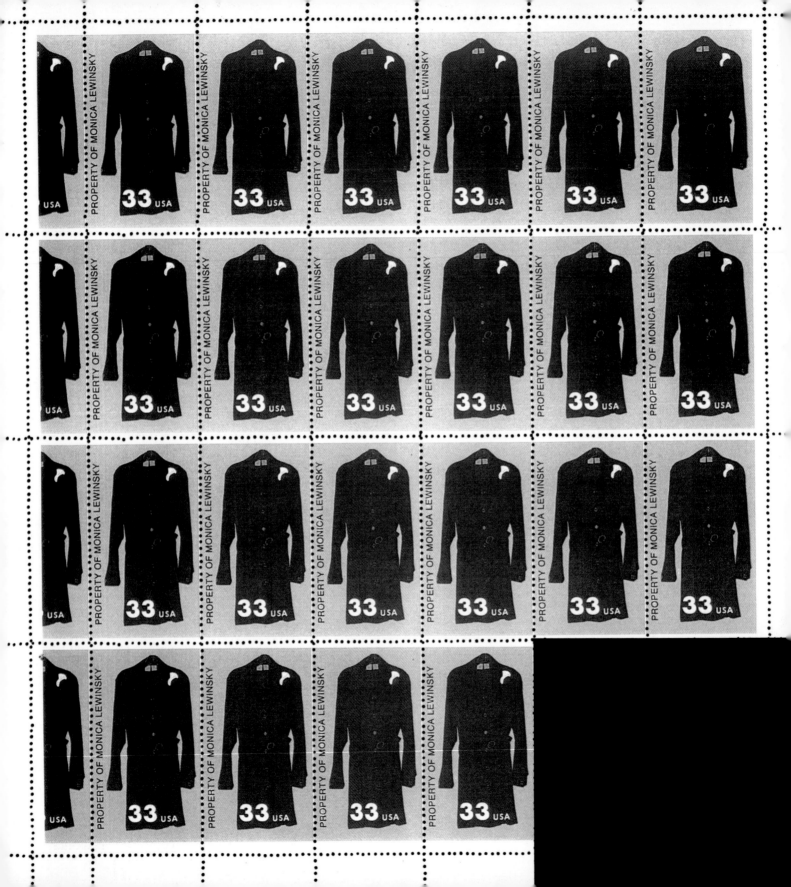

PROPERTY OF MONICA LEWINSKY

PROPERTY OF MONICA LEWINSKY

33 USA

33 USA

CAROL STREAM, IL

Mathias Seyl
Lenau Str 49
60318 Frankfurt aM

FOREIGN / GERMANY

Bill Clinton
Washington, DC

OFFICIAL BUSINESS

AIR
MAIL

MHDL

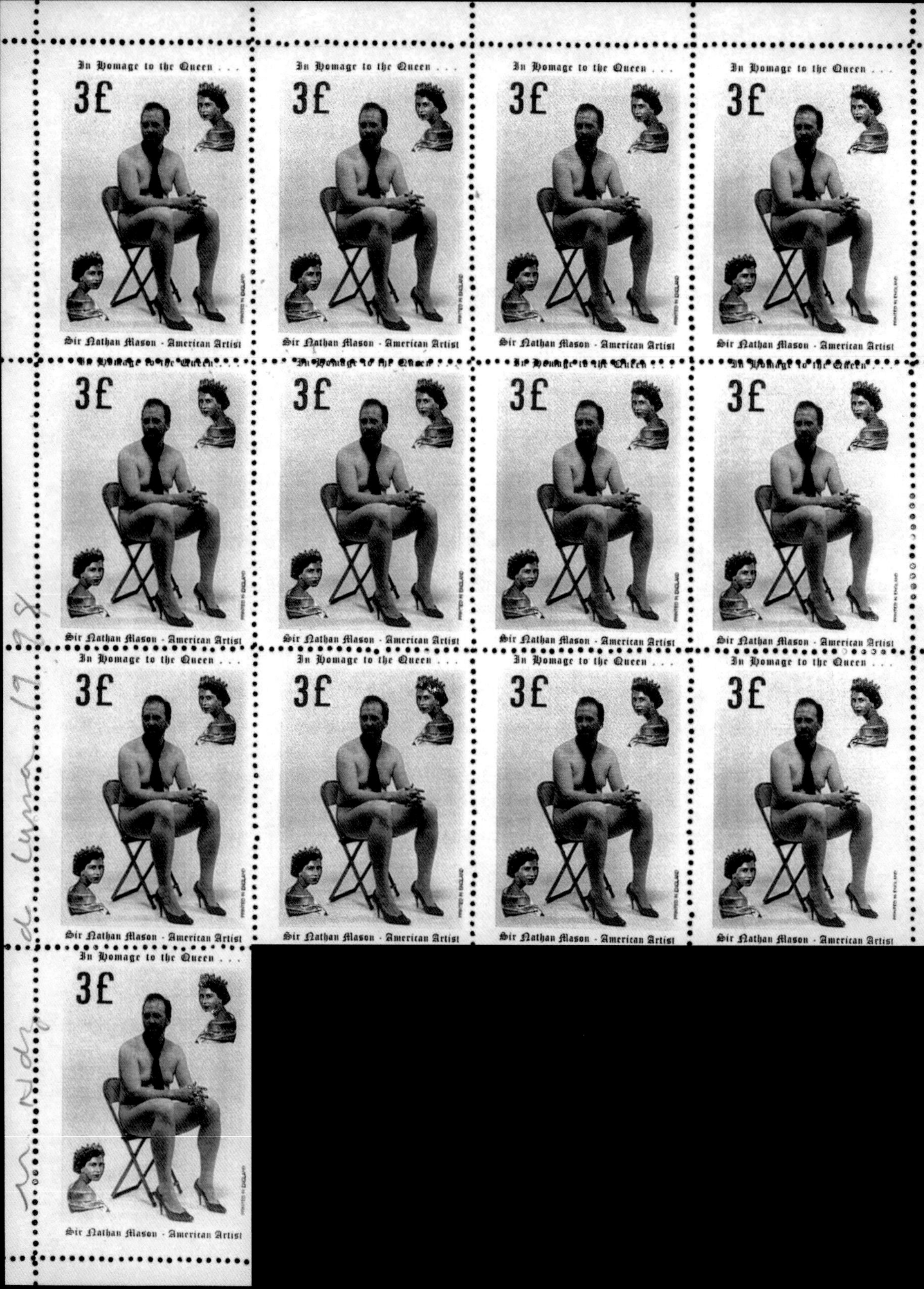
In Homage to the Queen . . .
3£
Sir Nathan Mason - American Artist

An Homage to the Queen

Postage 3£

Sir Nathan Mason - American Artist

PRINTED IN ENGLAND

3£ 29 NOV 199

VIA AEREA

The Renaissance Society

M. H. D. L. 1715 S. Laflin Chgo, IL 60608

60647/5502

US/

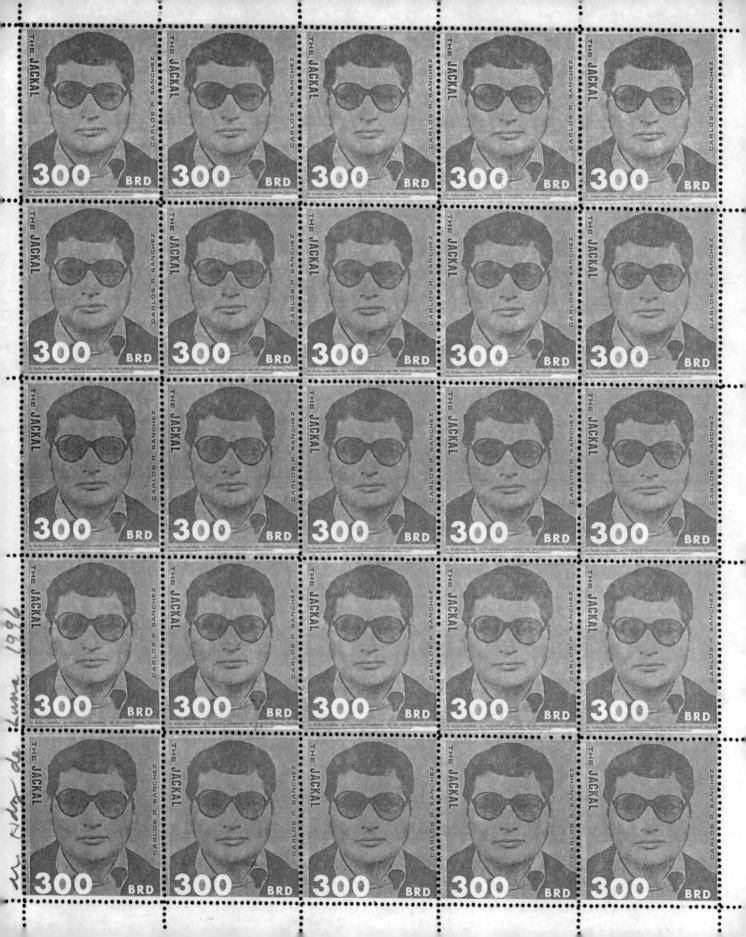

CARLOS R. SANCHEZ
THE **JACKAL**
300 BRD

CARLOS R. SANCHEZ
THE **JACKAL**
300 BRD

Mr. Michael Ndz de Luna
1441 W. 18th Str
Chicago Il. 60608
usa

60608/3035

VOTE Bill's Party Train... 33 USA

VOTE Bill's Party Train 33 USA

G E R M A N Y

C. Friesewinkel c/o M.H.D.L. Kaufunger str 24 60486 Frankfurt aM

AIRMAIL Fly Capital Airlines Constellations

AIRMAIL Fly Capital Airlines Constellations

AIRMAIL Fly Capital Airlines Constellations

RETURN IN FIVE DAYS TO

HOTEL SCHROEDER MILWAUKEE

00143/0000

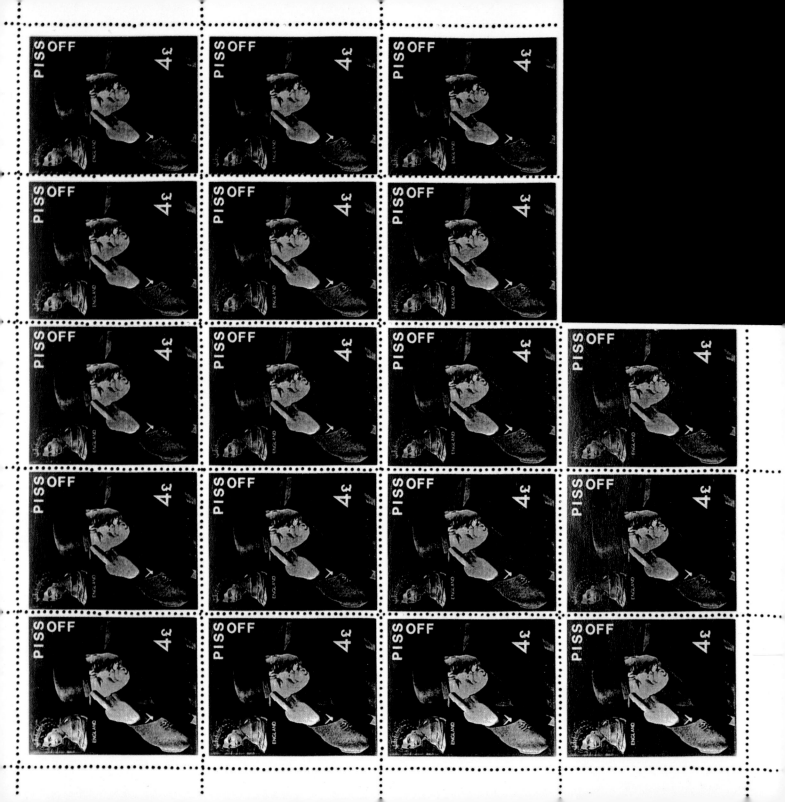

1999 — **British cancellation**

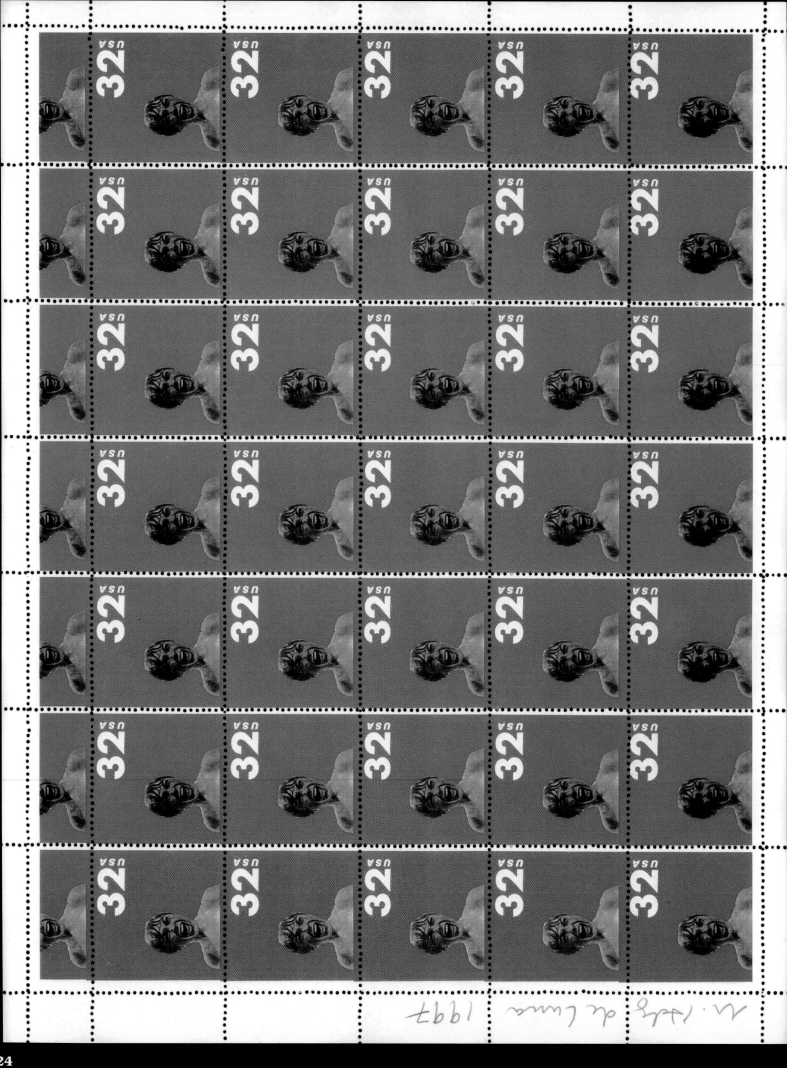

32 USA 32 USA

32 USA 32 USA

VIA AIR MAIL

CAROL STREAM P&DC IL 601,603 21

POSTAGE

M. SEYL

LENAU STR 49
60318 FRANKFURT

G E R M A N Y

Michael Hernandez de Luna
Frankenallee 108 A / 60326 Frankfurt
GERMANY

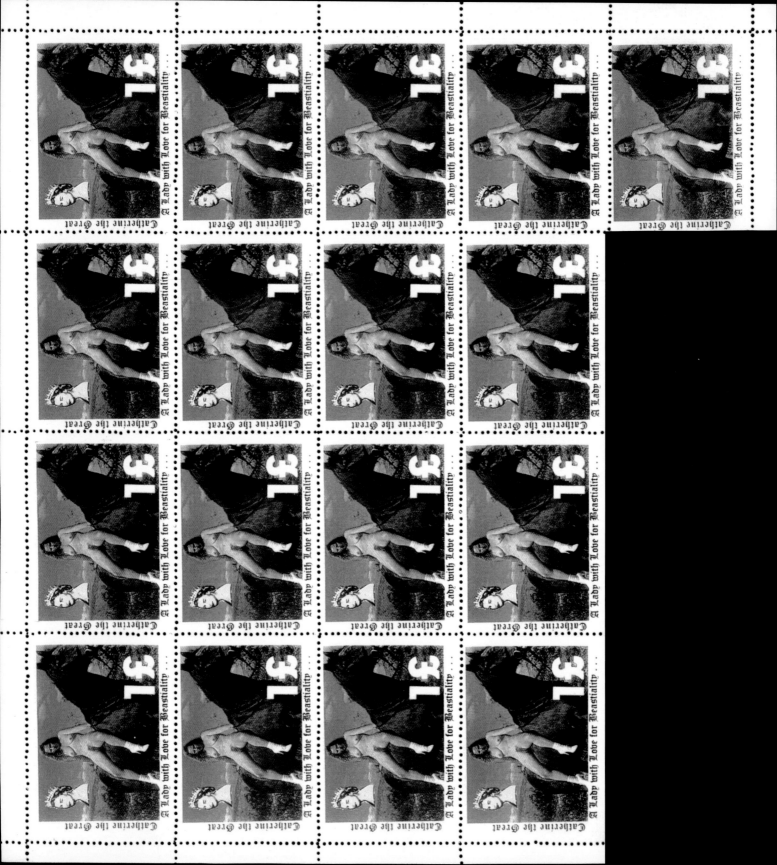

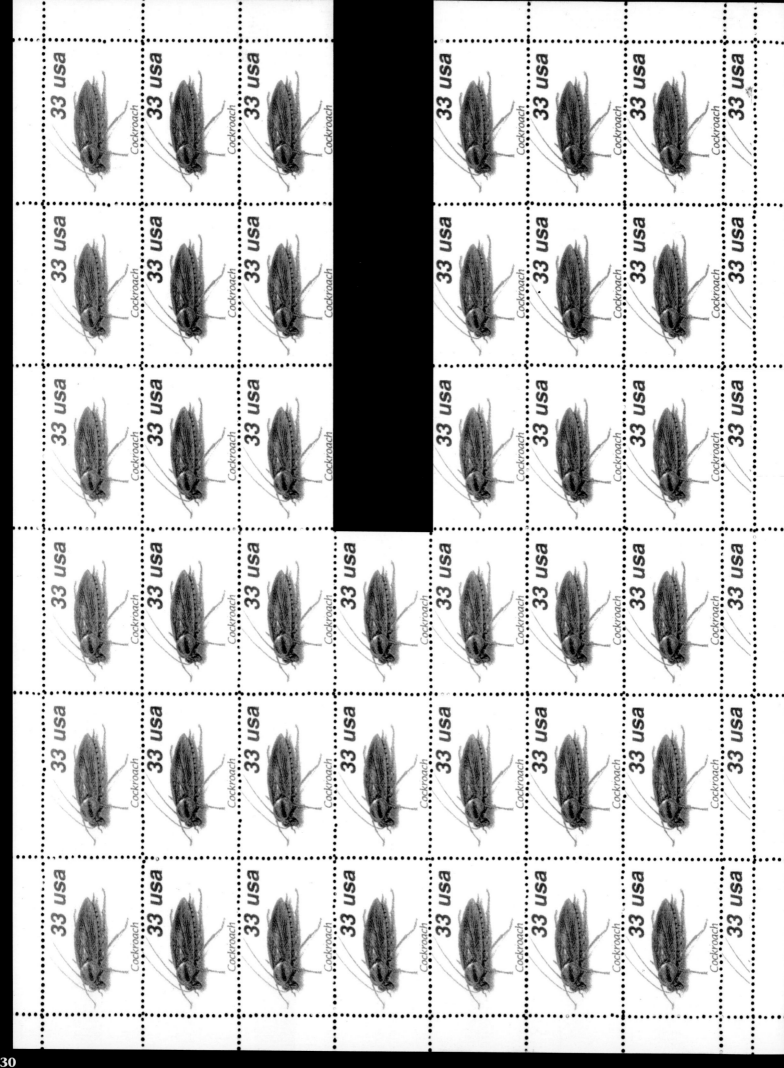

30

33 usa — Cockroach

33 usa — Cockroach

33 usa — Cockroach

35388

Michael Hernandez de Luna
Michael Hernandez de Luna Studio
1715 South Laflin
Chicago, IL 60608

Quaker 100% Natural Oats & Honey Cereal

Campbell's CHICKEN VEGETABLE

10 Foods you should never eat!

elf Portrait as a Conceptual artist. Die Kakamacher (the shitmaker) — 1998 — German Cancellation

Jesus was just a man & Mary was just a woman/Love 2 — 1997

TO: MHDL
608 2nd Ave
Seattle WA
98104

La idea de Luna 1986

138

65 Correos

Cuba

HAVANAS JFK

CUBAN

13.07.96

CUBA

HABANA I CP

MHDL

1441 West 18th

CHGO IL 60608

USA

60608+3035

— 1996 — Cuban cancellation

M. Ivès de Luxe 1998

M H D I
9
FRANCE

M. SEYL
c/o M. H. D. L.
Lenau Str. 49
60318 Frankfurt
GERMANY

POR AVION

D

UNIDOS

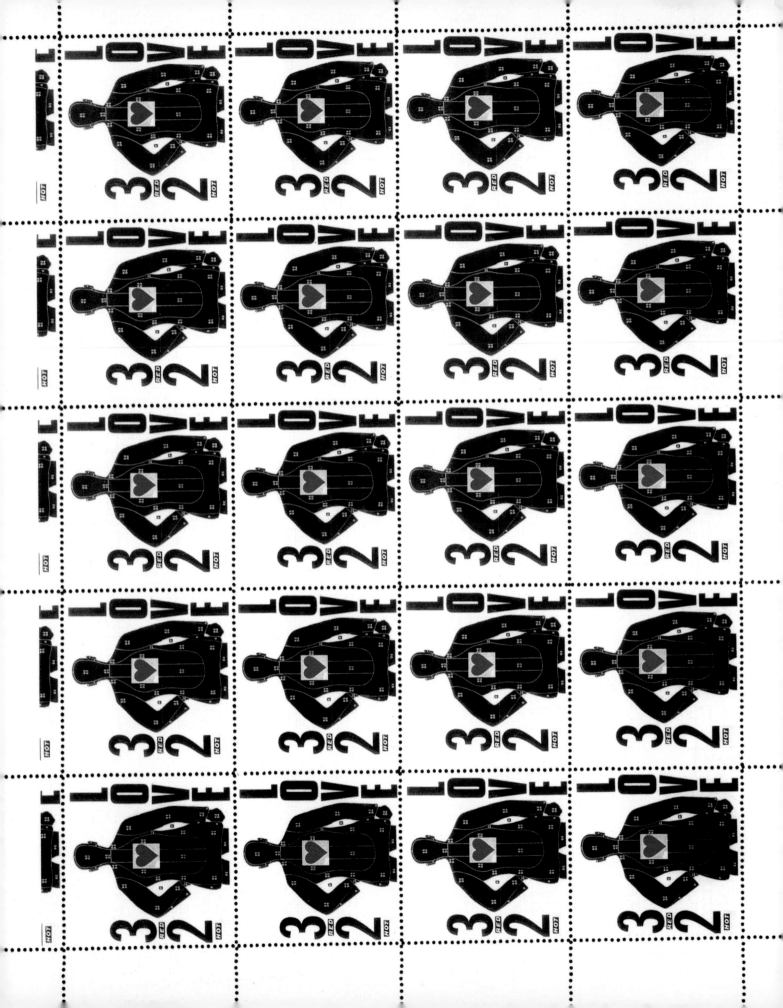

LOVE
LOVE
LOVE

IRVING PARK ROAD
USPS
HOT

M. Luna Love#3 -Reichel 43 60431 Frankfurt aM GERMANY

AIR
MAIL

FOR FAST SERVICE, USE

NORTHEAST AIRLINES

AIR
M. MAIL

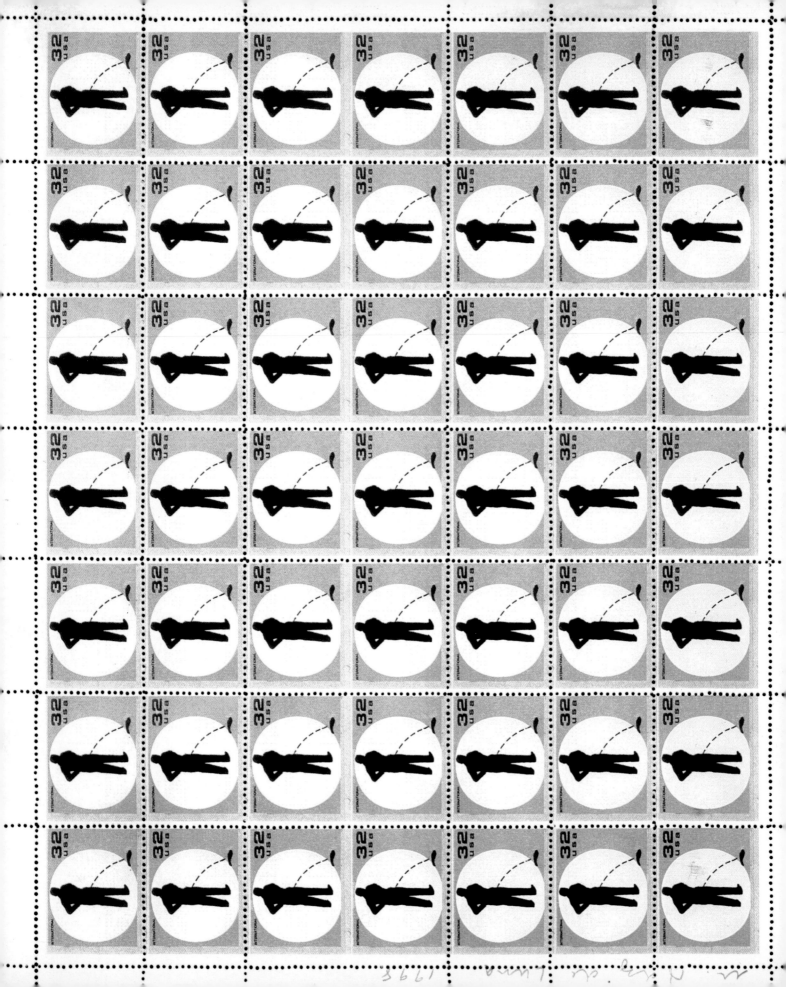

MHDL 1441 W. 18th Str. CHGO, IL. 60608 U. S. A.

Michael Hernandez de Luna
1441 W 18th Street
Chgo, IL 60608

60608-3035 27

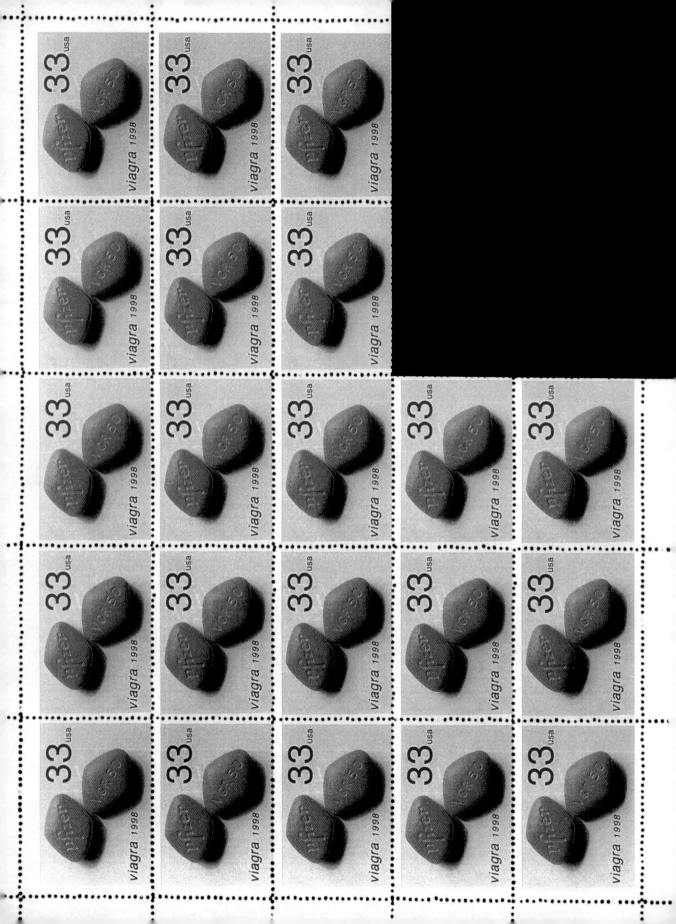

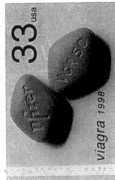

Di_____
Dep_____ of
CB#3_____amil_____
U. of _____th Ca_____
Chapel _ill, _
Applicant: Hu_____
Program: Soci_____

60608/2124

國立陽明醫學院
NATIONAL YANG-MING MEDICAL COLLEGE
Pei-Tou, Taipei, Taiwan 112
Republic of China

RUSH

Mr. M. Hong de lune
1715 S. Laflin
Chicago IL. 60608

1999 — Hong Kong cancellation

AIR MAIL

MHDL

Mathias Seyl
Lenau Str 49
60318 Frankfurt aM

FOREIGN / GERMANY

(IL), Morlen Sinoway Atelier / Morlen & Susan (IL), Mexican Fine Arts Center Museum / Rebecca Meyer & Cesáreo Moreno (IL), Museo de Filatelia / Alejandra Mora (MEX.), University of Guanjuato / Alejandro Flores (Mex.), Jack Tilton Gallery (NY), Wright Museum of Art (WI), Meredith Kelly Gallery / Mary & Cat (NM), Pearl Conard Gallery (OH), Printmakers Collaborative (IL), Glass Curtain Gallery (IL), Kougeas Gallery (MA), Hyde Park Art Center (IL), Noyes Art Center (IL), Judy Saslow Gallery (IL), Chicago Compex (IL), ARC Gallery (IL), The Greg Kucera Gallery (WA), Lovely Fine Art (IL), UIC 400 Gallery (IL), The Betty Rymer Gallery (IL), VU Gallery (WA), The Columbia College Gallery (IL), Guadalupe Fine Art (NM), Los Manos Gallery (IL), Hotwired / Sarah Borruso (CA), Details (NY), Playboy / Terri Glover (IL), The Face / Gemma Booth (UK), The News (Mex.), The San Francisco Chronicle / Leah Garchick & Amy Linn (CA), Linns Stamp News (OH), Scotts Monthly Stamp News / Peter Martin (OH), The Chicago Reader (IL), New City / Frank Sennett (IL), Deutsch GQ (D) The Chicago Tribune / John O'Brien & Jon Anderson / INC: Hevrdejs & Conklin (IL), Blender (DK), Juxtapoz / Jamie O'Shea (CA), Anodyne (OR), The Oregonian (OR), Willamette Weekly / D. Row (OR), Santa Fe New Mexican / K. McCloud (NM), Metropolis / Mark Spiegler (NY), Associated Press / Tara Burghard, Third Word (IL), WIRED (CA), 10 X 10 (IL), EXITO (IL), Telemundo TV (FL), WGN TV (IL), WPWR Radio (IL), Fox TV (IL), CLTV (IL), CNN, Wild Chicago (IL), Artistamp News / Ed Varney (CANADADA), Illinois Arts Council (IL), Joe Fontana, Dan DeRuiter, Frank Kreft, France Kozlik, Evelyn Daitchman, Michael Lumb, Alan Turner, Gianni Simone, Dada Kan, Alan Palmer, Floyd Gomph, Robin Richman, Shane & Jody Kennedy, Kelly Thompson & Don, Skipper & Pam Thompson, Steven & Sue Thompson, Mr. & Mrs. R.W. Thompson, Alfonso y Consuelo Hernández de Luna, Bella de Luna y the Hernández siblings, Deborah, Jessica, y Joey Menchaca, JoJo DiCarlo, Doug Huston, Suzanne Endsley, Mary y Roy Cullen, Michael & Inez Brunner, Eleazar y Sylvia Delgado, Marcus Winter, Umberto, Felicetta y Adel Ricco, Jeff Levine, Kevin Conway, Lisa Fransico, Steve Edelman, Courtney Lance, Diedra Baumann, Brian Bonebrake, Charles Berg, Jim Ashby (The Stamp Man), John Rininger, Todd Snapp, Mathais y Anabel Seyl, Teresa y Claudia Molnar, Marion Ortwein, John Mason, Mindy Rezman, Siegmar Jeromin, Larry Yellen y Sue Fisher, Chuck Thurow, The Golden Boys of Manitoba: Roland Bertram y Ike Hoemann, Henry Fan & Hee Chung Kim, Thaddeus y Mary Kay Staton-Long, Jane Kozuch y David Berten, Marla Mason, Victor y Mayte Harbison, Sven von Brasch, Raul Ross, Dr. Nelson Borelli, Bert Meyer, Geraldo Yepiz, Arnaldo y Lulu Cohen, Liska Blodgett, Ludwig Zeller y Suzanna Wald, Freddy Mata, Karl Hammer, Michael Howell, Mike Pocius, Ryosuke Cohen, Richard Loya, Ristomatti Ratia, Joan Shenk, Picasso Gaglione, Glenn Joffe, Stanley Gallas, Sallie Gratch, Gael Grayson, Carolyn y Gretchen Rudy, Vittore Baroni, Mary Ann Redding, Emmet O'Conner, Don Gessig, Los StraightJackets, Ada Blacey, Laura Bryant, Marcus Casa Madrid, Mark Ernst, Nathan Mason, Marty Mroz, Monica Rezman, John Phillips y Jo Hormuth, Ivan Stankowicz, Dirk Wales, NEWARTNOW.com,, Mi Wu, Danih Jaras, Vyto B., Jose Andreu, Baby Doll, Keith y Sayad Walker, Rudy y Lety Avina, Angelo y Denise Varias, Nick De Genova, Eric & Jessica Greenberg-Bruozis, Judith & Aubrey Greenberg, Karen & Tom Uhlmann, Bruce Doblin, Guy y Marilyn Revesz, Nobert Zook, Dee Dee Gross, Maury Ettleson, Bob Sirot, Alan Pocius, Nora Chiriboga, Heriberto Rodriguez, Milton Rodriguez, Pete Rodriguez, Aida Rodriguez, y Ricky Moreno, Joel Rendon, Victor Cassidy, Jeff y Hector Maldonado, Laurens Grant, Tiffani Sorber, Angel the Spaniard, Nancy Benjamin, Tracy Ostmann, Tim Brown y Jill Ridell, Lauren Moltz y John Clement, Jas Felter, Tim Dashnaw, Martin Geise ∎

BADPRESSBOOKS.COM